"THE POSSIBLE DREAM is the living success story of thousands of Americans today."

—Success Unlimited

The dream of Rich DeVos and Jay Van Andel was to build a company that would offer all persons who seek it a chance to change their lives. Amway offers a way for the average person to *try* to make things better. It offers a dream—and not just a dream—but a *possible* dream.

"Who sells Amway products and why do they do it? Just about every imaginable sort of person does...Amway is profoundly American...wrapping itself in the virtues of patriotism, free enterprise and positive thinking."

—The New York Times

Berkley Books by Charles Paul Conn

AN UNCOMMON FREEDOM
BELIEVE! (With Richard M. DeVos)
THE POSSIBLE DREAM
THE WINNER'S CIRCLE
PROMISES TO KEEP

About the **Author:**

Charles Paul Conn is an award-winning freelance writer whose books about sports, politics, entertainment, religion, and the business world have appeared on every major bestseller list in America. In addition to THE WINNER'S CIRCLE, which was a *New York Times* bestseller, he has also written THE NEW JOHNNY CASH, THE POSSIBLE DREAM, BATTLE FOR AFRICA, KATHY, FATHERCARE, MAKING IT HAPPEN, and AN UNCOMMON FREEDOM. Conn holds a Ph.D. in psychology from Emory University in Atlanta, Georgia, and was a Visiting Scholar at Harvard University.

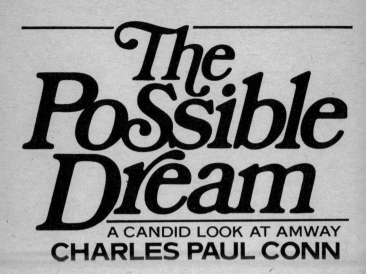

The Possible Dream

A CANDID LOOK AT AMWAY

CHARLES PAUL CONN

BERKLEY BOOKS, NEW YORK

This Berkley book contains the complete
text of the original hardcover edition.
It has been completely reset in a typeface
designed for easy reading and was printed
from new film.

THE POSSIBLE DREAM

A Berkley Book / published by arrangement with
Fleming H. Revell Company

PRINTING HISTORY
Fleming H. Revell edition published 1977
Berkley edition / May 1978

ISBN: 0-425-10566-0

A BERKLEY BOOK ® TM 757,375
Berkley Books are published by The Berkley Publishing Group,
200 Madison Avenue, New York, New York 10016.
The name "Berkley" and the "B" logo
are trademarks belonging to Berkley Publishing Corporation.

PRINTED IN THE UNITED STATES OF AMERICA

50 49 48 47 46 45 44 43 42

TO DARLIA,
my wife,
and the very best person I know

Contents

Preface

What in the world is Amway?

It is a business, of course—one that manufactures and sells household products, soaps, toothpaste, and cosmetics. But for many people, it obviously is much more than just a business. For some, it seems to be a consuming involvement that shapes conservative political views—one that has young couples saluting the American flag who, a few years ago, were demonstrating against LBJ's war and the whole bag of capitalistic values. One newspaper called Amway a "prepackaged way of life." A leading national magazine called it "a socioreligious phenomenon of some sort." And some of its corporate officials declare, unblinkingly, that all that is so much pseudopsychological fluff—that Amway, in fact, is a business and nothing else—that it has to do with products and profits, plain and simple.

Just what is Amway, anyway?

The company's promotional literature refers to "The World of Amway" and this book is a look at that world. I first became interested in writing a book about Amway almost three years back, and began gathering materials at that time. In early 1977, the president and chairman of the board of Amway agreed to grant me access to the records and activities of the company, to make themselves and other corporate personnel available for interviews, and to cooperate fully with my investigation of this "World of Amway."

They have been true to that promise, and in these nine months I have examined the company's operation at every level. I have traveled seventy thousand miles to interview fifty-plus individuals; have attended Amway meetings of varying sizes in three dozen cities literally from Maine to Los Angeles, San Juan to Vancouver; have talked to winners and losers—and some who aren't sure yet. Amway's corporate leaders, from the top down, have given me a free hand, and generous amounts of their own time, and have never attempted to control the editorial outcome. This is a book that could not have been written without that cooperation, and I am indebted to them for it.

"Just call 'em like you see 'em," President Richard DeVos told me when I started the project. I have done that in the text which follows. What I have written is *my* view of the company, and the Amway Corporation is in no way responsible for the observations or conclusions that emerge. The company itself has a strict policy of recognizing its distributors solely on the basis of their level of achievement in the business, but I have not been bound by this policy and have not attempted to observe it. No company official has suggested whom I should interview or write about, and I have made editorial decisions based on the features of the story which emerged naturally as I worked.

There is a series of Amway magazine ads which bear the slogan "Amway...get the *whole* story." I have tried to get that story, and this book describes it the way I found it to be.

Today, the story of Amway is just as timely as when the book was first written. Various statistical data and other technical information have been changed to update the text of this edition. The "dream" itself has not changed; it seems destined to grow and expand into the 1980's.

CHARLES PAUL CONN

February 1982

1 Partners

In 1940 Adolf Hitler invaded Holland, Belgium, and France. Not personally, of course. (That wasn't Hitler's style. One could get hurt that way.) His soldiers actually did the invading, wave after wave of them—crack troops sweeping through to Paris almost as fast as their Panzer tanks could carry them.

Nineteen forty was also the year that *Gone With the Wind* won an armful of Oscars at the Academy Award ceremonies, and lines of people waiting to see it outside theatres grew even longer. The helicopter was developed that year; its first flight lasted a full fifteen minutes. And nylon stockings were placed on sale for the first time. Women stormed the counters of clothing stores in every major city, and even with a two-pair-per-customer limit, the entire supply of seventy-two thousand pairs in New York City sold out in eight hours. The Cincinnati Reds, on the strong pitching of Johnny Vander Meer, beat the Detroit Tigers in a seven-game World Series at old Crosley Field, in what was still the lily-white game of baseball. And in a somewhat more serious contest, Franklin D. Roosevelt audaciously ran for an unprecedented third term as president, and clobbered Republican Wendell Willkie at the polls.

Gasoline cost ten cents a gallon. The Golden Gate Bridge was just completed, a new attraction for San Francisco gawkers; television was still a laboratory fantasy; and Joe Louis was in his early prime, virtually unchallenged in boxing as heavy-weight champion of the world.

It was also in 1940 that a serious young teenager at Christian High School in Grand Rapids, Michigan, found a way to offset the expense of driving to school. The student was Jay Van Andel, age sixteen. He came from a large Dutch community in Grand Rapids, and had ridden a bicycle to school for years—quite a distance from the south side of town—because it was important for him to attend the school, which is owned and operated by members of the Christian Reformed Church. But the winters can be rough on bicyclists in Grand Rapids, and when his family moved to the north side of town—to a neighborhood even farther from Christian High—his father had bought him an old Model *A* Ford.

Now he had help with the gas money. A fellow student had approached him that day—a younger boy who lived about three blocks from Jay's house—and asked if they might make a deal. His name was Rich DeVos. "I didn't know him," Van Andel recalls, "but I had noticed him before. He was in one of my classes and for some reason I remember being aware of him and being attracted to him." DeVos made an offer: "If you'll give me a ride to school and back, I'll pay twenty-five cents a week toward the gas. Your car, my gas money." It was a good deal for both boys. DeVos, who had been riding the bus every day, now had transportation; and Van Andel, who had paid the cost of driving alone, now had a partner.

The arrangement they made that day was a good one; and today, forty years later, Jay Van Andel and Rich DeVos are still riding side-by-side—not in a Model A Ford these days, but at the head of Amway Corporation. Amway is one of America's most intriguing companies, and surely one of the most interesting stories of partnership and success in recent economic history. Since 1940, the battles of World War II, Korea, and Vietnam have come and gone; ten different presidents have occupied the White House; *Gone With the Wind* has gone and returned again; nylon stockings have given way to panty hose; Crosley Field has been replaced by Riverfront Stadium; and Joe Louis has watched from ringside as the likes of Marciano and Liston and Ali have fought for his crown.

But a few things have endured. The Golden Gate Bridge hasn't changed. Helicopters and television are still around. And Rich DeVos and Jay Van Andel have endured—not merely endured but prospered, not only individually, but together, as a team. Operating with a finely tuned communication that only they understand, they jointly conduct the affairs of one of America's top twenty-five privately owned companies, with little more to guide them than a handshake and a gentleman's agreement. It is more than one could have expected from two teenaged buddies driving to school together every morning in a Model *A* Ford.

Rich DeVos is fond of saying that men make very few big decisions in life, that strings of small, insignificant decisions usually carry men in the paths their lives take.

His own liaison with Jay Van Andel over the years is a perfect example of that point. From their first agreement to share a ride to school, the friendship grew by small steps, finally becoming a relationship of enormous importance, directly affecting hundreds of thousands of people and hundreds of millions of dollars each year. The two men are, in a sense, inextricably bound to one another by a web of circumstance and shared interests. They are the ultimate example of businessmen-partners, and much is made of the rare way in which they complement one another—the remarkable degree to which their separate skills and inclinations mesh in an efficient working whole. But it is important to remember that they were not selected for one another by a computer, each drawn for the way his own set of counterbalancing qualities fits the other. They did not set out with calculating forethought to put together a two-man executive superteam. It surely seems to have worked out that way, but in the beginning they were just two schoolboys who enjoyed being together. "Sometimes people forget," Van Andel says, "that Rich and I got together because we liked each other. That's all. We became partners simply because we liked each other. We enjoyed being together."

The summer after they met, the young friends embarked on a trip that DeVos calls "the first significant thing we ever did on our own." Van Andel's father ran a garage and had sold two used pickup trucks to be delivered to Montana. He offered to let the boys drive them out to Montana for him. Rich's mother went to talk with Jay's father to work out the details; and when school adjourned, the two boys departed Grand Rapids—at ages sixteen and fourteen—for the Far West. They took a tent and camped out along the way, stretching the four-thousand-mile trip into a three-week excursion through the West.

They had their little frustrations. Once, just outside the Yellowstone National Park, they had three blowouts simultaneously on one of the trucks. They were on the side of the road immediately adjacent to a service station, but had no money to spare, so they pulled a tire-repair kit from the back of the truck and patched the tires themselves. The station operator, irritated because they hadn't hired him to repair the tires, refused to let them have "free air" from his air hose. He intended to squeeze a nickel or two out of them, one way or another. He should have known better. The two good Dutch boys sat tight, waiting until they could borrow an old hand pump from a passing motorist, pumped up their own tires, and went their way not a penny poorer.

DeVos and Van Andel eventually reached Montana, delivered the trucks, and came home on a Greyhound bus. It was quite an adventure for two boys who hadn't begun shaving yet, and today both men point to the trip as the occasion that cemented their friendship.

When World War II engulfed the United States,

DeVos and Van Andel each enlisted for military service. Both entered the air corps and served until the end of the war. They stayed in touch during those years, and on one occasion were home on leave at the same time. It was then that they first talked seriously about going into business together after the war.

One Sunday night, just before each was to leave Grand Rapids to return to duty, they sat up late at night, talked about the future, and agreed to open "some sort of business" together.

"Some sort of business" turned out to be the Wolverine Air Service, a flying school and air-charter service at Comstock Park, near Grand Rapids. Van Andel was discharged from the corps several months before DeVos, so he took the lead in establishing the business. DeVos, still overseas, wrote his father and asked him to give Van Andel seven hundred dollars—his total savings—for half the start-up cost of the business.

By the time DeVos returned to Grand Rapids, the flying school was almost ready to operate. DeVos picks up the story: "We hit a snag. When we got our customers signed up and our instructors hired, we discovered that the runways at the little airport had not been completed yet. They were still nothing but giant streaks of mud. We improvised. A river ran alongside the airport, so we bought some floats for our Piper Cub and flew right off the water, taking off and landing on those pontoon floats. We were supposed to have offices there at the little airstrip, but they weren't built in time for our opening. Jay bought a chicken coop from a farmer down the road, hauled it over to the airstrip, whitewashed it, and hung a sign that read grandly: WOLVERINE AIR SERVICE. We were in business!"

One thing led to another. The partners, apparently concluding that the aviation business left them with too much idle time on their hands, opened a hamburger stand in a prefab building which they erected at the airstrip. It had a one-man kitchen and spaces for cars to park—an early Grand Rapids version of what would later be called a "drive-in restaurant." On opening day the power company reported they couldn't deliver electricity on schedule, so the rookie restauranteurs rented a portable generator and opened on time anyway. The division of labor was simple: DeVos grilled hamburgers while Van Andel "hopped" cars, or Van Andel did hamburgers while DeVos did the cars. It worked out about the same either way. Both remember the restaurant experience without an excess of enthusiasm.

"Those early business experiences seem almost funny today," DeVos says, "but they worked. That was what mattered. If they hadn't been successful, maybe we would have gone our separate ways. Who knows? But we had a good time and we made some money, so we just kept rolling along together." After two years, they sold the businesses for a tidy profit, and decided it was time to reward themselves for their hard work with a bit of adventure on the high seas.

They got perhaps a bit more adventure than they planned.

They pooled their money once again and sank it—perhaps an unfortunate choice of words—into an old thirty-eight-foot schooner called *Elizabeth*. In December of 1948, they set sail from Norwalk, Connecticut, for a year-long cruise in the Atlantic Ocean. They planned to sail down the East Coast of the United States, through the Caribbean, and eventually down the coast of South

America. They were going to learn to sail as they went, of course, since neither of them had ever been sailing on a boat before! The first hint that they were in over their heads (pardon the expression) came long before they reached the Caribbean, as DeVos remembers it:

"We got a few quick lessons and set sail with the book in one hand and the tiller in the other. We got lost immediately. We got lost so badly in New Jersey that even the U.S. Coast Guard couldn't find us. We missed two turns at night and got way back up in the inland marshes someplace. When the coast guard finally found us, after an all-day search, they couldn't believe where we were. 'Nobody has ever been this far inland in a boat this size before,' they told us, and hauled us back out to the ocean with a rope."

But Van Andel and DeVos learned fast. In a few weeks they were sailing and navigating with a reasonable amount of skill, but, as luck would have it, by the time they finally learned what they were doing, the *Elizabeth* began to leak. One dark night in March as they sailed from Havana, bound for Haiti, the leaky old hull finally gave up the ghost, and the schooner sank in fifteen hundred feet of water, ten miles off the northern coast of Cuba. The two sailors were rescued by an American freighter called the *Addabell Lydes*, which dropped them a few days later in San Juan, Puerto Rico.

Both men vow that it never seriously occurred to them to turn back. They wired home to assure their parents they were safe and to arrange to collect insurance benefits on their ill-fated schooner, then struck out again. They spent five months traveling through the islands, and on to Central and South America before finally, their "vacation" ended, returning to Grand Rapids.

Those were carefree, madcap days for Van Andel and DeVos. They were both unmarried, debt-free, and in a perfect situation to take a chance, sink a ship, look for hidden treasure, or whatever else they wanted to do. But by the time they got home, they were hungry again, not for adventure this time, but for achievement—for accomplishments of substance and permanence. They went into business together again the very month they returned from South America, and this time their business lives began to focus more tightly in ways which hinted at things to come.

2 A Beginning

An unsolicited visit from a distant relative is rarely an occasion of great rejoicing.

It was such a visit that got DeVos and Van Andel off and running in the business careers they had talked about for so many years. The distant relative was a second cousin of Van Andel's, a fiftyish Dutch immigrant named Neil Maaskant. He lived in Chicago, and called to tell cousin Jay that he had started a new business, asking if he could drive up to Grand Rapids to talk about it.

It was August, 1949. The two friends had just returned from South America and were ready to settle down and work, so the timing was right for them. "Sure, why not?" they answered. It couldn't hurt to hear what he had to say. They had bought a cottage on Brower Lake, a few miles outside Grand Rapids—a twenty-four-by-twenty-foot building—and it was here Maaskant came to make his sales pitch, accompanied by Van Andel's father and mother. Before they arrived, DeVos decided to find something more entertaining to do for the evening, and left the cottage. "They're your relatives," he told Jay. "*You* talk to them!"

So Jay talked to them. When Rich returned to the cabin at midnight, Jay was still talking to them. And they kept right on talking until after 2:00 A.M. When the visitors finally departed, the names of Rich DeVos and Jay Van Andel were on the dotted line, at the bottom of an application form. They were distributors of a line of food supplements called *Nutrilite Products*, with all the rights, honors, and privileges thereunto appertaining.

Nutrilite Products was a California-based direct-sales company. *Direct sales* meant simply that its goods were marketed by individual distributors who sold directly to their customers. Van Andel and DeVos were not familiar with that phrase; and before that evening in 1949, they might have referred to the Nutrilite plan as a "door-to-door" operation. The "door-to-door" tag, strictly speaking, does not apply either to the Nutrilite operation of 1949 or to the Amway plan of today. *Direct sales* means that a product is sold person-to-person, but not necessarily door-to-door.

A direct-sales business may not have been exactly what the two partners were looking for, but when they heard the Nutrilite sales plan explained, it sounded easy enough to them. Maaskant had shown them his commission check and it was a pretty hefty amount. They reasoned that if he, a middle-aged immigrant still with a thick

Dutch accent, could make big money in the business, certainly they could do as well. So they signed up. The product they were selling was a box of Nutrilite food supplement capsules, a month's supply costing $19.50, and the next day they sold to their first customer. "He was an old man who ran a beer-and-wine, pick-up grocery on the lake nearby," DeVos recalls. "We asked him to buy a box and he did, just because he liked us. After we made that one sale, we didn't do another thing for two weeks."

What turned things around two weeks later was a trip to Chicago to a meeting of Nutrilite distributors. Maaskant had urged them to attend, so they drove to Chicago to see what they had gotten into. The meeting was at a downtown hotel, and over one hundred people were there. They heard a fellow named Lee Mytinger speak, saw a film on Nutrilite products, and talked to people who had been distributors for several years. Everything they saw and heard made a favorable impression. On the way back to Grand Rapids that night, throughout the long, five-hour trip, they kicked the Nutrilite idea around, and by the time they reached the outskirts of town, they had made the decision to go all the way with the Nutrilite opportunity. They stopped at a gas station on the way into town and sold the station attendant a box of Nutrilite, and the ball was rolling.

The Nutrilite business was a fairly simple one. A distributor gave his friend or neighbor a copy of a booklet (title: "How to Get Well and Stay Well") describing the need for food supplements, or perhaps made an appointment to make a more elaborate presentation to him personally. If the distributor could convince the individual of the need for a dietary supplement, he made a customer of him, supplying him with a box of food supplement tablets (Nutrilite "XX") each month for $19.50. The principle on which Nutrilite products was based was that of concentrating large amounts of green material (alfalfa, watercress, and parsley) which were not cooked or refined, and adding them to the diet in tablet form. It was not a difficult product to sell. (Van Andel and DeVos began eating "XX" when they became Nutrilite distributors, and have continued to do so regularly until the present time.) The system in those days required new distributors to sell twenty-five customers before they were eligible to sponsor other distributors. DeVos remembers that this twenty-fifth customer was a home designer named Randy Cooper, who was an army buddy of Jay's. DeVos sold him the product, and then tried to interest him in becoming a distributor himself, but Cooper was not so inclined. "I can remember that night very clearly, in a little house in southeast Grand Rapids," DeVos says. One of life's small ironies is that Cooper, who is still a friend of DeVos and Van Andel, was sponsored into Amway only a few years ago.

On their next sponsoring try, DeVos and Van Andel had better luck. They invited a friend out to their cottage on the lake, read him the marketing plan word-for-word from the sales manual, and sponsored him. He quit a few weeks later, but still it was a beginning. They worked hard and grew rapidly. Within several months they had built one of the most successful distributorships in the Nutrilite business.

It wasn't all smooth water. They held their first public meeting for prospective distributors in the basement of a little restaurant at the old Grand Rapids airport. They

14

had placed an ad in the paper and hoped for a good response. Only eight people showed. They all came together, marched to the front row, and sat down. Jay gave a little welcoming speech and showed a film about nutrition, then Rich gave a closing pitch and invited "all who are interested" to stay and talk over the business. All eight people stood up and marched out. They didn't say hello-good-bye-boo-or-kiss-my-foot. They just walked out. About five minutes later, as the two partners were glumly packing up their projector and sales material, one of the eight came back in the door. "My wife made me come back to explain to you guys," he said. "We are in the Nutrilite business already, and we just wanted to see what you young fellows were up to." And with that he was gone. That discouraged them even more. They hadn't known anyone else was selling Nutrilite in the Grand Rapids area, and wondered whether or not there would be room for them to build the business there in the same town.

There were good days, too. Outstanding distributors started coming out of the woodwork, providing leadership of their own, widening the circle of contacts. They opened a small office on Eastern Avenue in Grand Rapids. New people began to come aboard who would be with them twenty-five years later: a Dale Carnegie instructor named Walter Bass; a shy housewife named Eleanor Tietsma (who began as a customer and started sponsoring almost despite herself); a barber named Fred Hansen who moved to Akron, Ohio, and started a strong distributorship there.

Fred Hansen's widow, Bernice, is still an active Amway leader in Ohio. She remembers those early days:

"We were back in Grand Rapids visiting when Fred heard about a new business, and went to a meeting to hear about it. He came back and I asked him what it was all about. 'Selling pills door-to-door,' he said. That sounded terrible. But a month later we learned more about it and got in. We were living in Akron, and Rich DeVos and Walter Bass drove all the way from Grand Rapids—325 miles—in an old Packard automobile. We had five couples there. I made a coffee cake and sent the kids upstairs, and Rich and Walt held the meeting. All five of those couples came into the business that night, and before he left, Rich reminded me that the money I had spent on that coffee cake was tax-deductible!" That was June of 1950. (Thirty years later, the Hansen distributorship is still a strong, lucrative business, and many Amway distributors fondly refer to the grandmotherly Mrs. Hansen as the "First Lady of Amway.")

Van Andel and DeVos were young and aggressive. As the business gathered momentum, they pushed even harder. People like Joe Victor, a milk-truck driver, built large distributorships rapidly, setting examples that motivated others. One distributor from those early days tells about becoming concerned when their sales volume dropped slightly one month. He wrote DeVos to complain about the distributors in his organization not working. He got a terse note back in reply: "Start working harder yourself and you'll set a better example." He did, and his volume went right back up again. But if the two young entrepreneurs accepted few excuses from their distributors, they also maintained a high standard for themselves.

DeVos reminisces about what it was like in those days.

"I remember one night in Lansing, Michigan, Jay and I had a big sales meeting. It was really going to be a dandy! We had been on radio with big ads, and had put notices in the papers. All day long we collared people and passed out brochures, revving up for a big meeting. We had an auditorium with two hundred seats, and that night two people showed up! Did you ever make a rock-'em-sock-'em sales speech to two people in a room with two hundred seats? And then drive home at two o'clock in the morning because you couldn't afford to pay those motel rates? You do one of two things: either you give up, or you persist. We persisted."

They not only persisted—they thrived. After two years in the Nutrilite business, things were going so well they decided to diversify. They began to organize other businesses. First they went into health foods. Encouraged by the many health-foods enthusiasts among their Nutrilite customers, they started a business called Stone Mill Products, a health-foods bakery that offered customers a "home-baked, stone-ground loaf of bread." They kept the new venture separate from the Nutrilite organization, distributing the bread through a truck-delivery service. The success of this venture led to a mail-order business for the Stone Mill goods, which quickly expanded to a mailing list of forty thousand names and addresses. Their next venture was a company to make wooden toys, specializing in rocking horses, which they called the Grand Rapids Toy Company. They lost their shirts on that one.

As they branched out into new ventures, the growth rate of their Nutrilite business began to sag slightly. They were concerned—not alarmed, but concerned—and made the decision to divest themselves of all other interests and concentrate solely on the Nutrilite distributorship. They sold the health foods and mail-order businesses at a profit, took a nice, healthy loss on the rocking horses, and poured their energies back into Nutrilite. Once again, the needle jumped. The growth rate moved up again. They had learned a lesson they wouldn't forget: Concentrate on a winner; don't diffuse your energy.

Unfortunately, things began to go badly for Nutrilite on a national scale. The problem was one of internal warfare. The company was actually two companies: Nutrilite Products Incorporated, which made the products; and Mytinger and Casselberry, which operated the distributor organization. The two companies had worked well together for years, but began to quarrel over many different problems, including whether to add a line of cosmetics to their food supplement products. Eventually the bickering erupted into full-scale warfare.

A study group composed of leading Nutrilite distributors tried to bring the warring factions together, but without success. Jay Van Andel had served as chairman of that group. "I flew from Michigan to the West Coast many times—and that was in propeller days—trying to help solve the problems," he recounts. "There seemed to be no solutions. Things had gone too far."

In early 1959, Carl Rehnborg, the founder of Nutrilite, came to Van Andel and offered him the job of president of the company. It was an enticing offer to the young businessman: a thirty-thousand-dollar-per-year salary, sudden elevation to the front office from the field, the presidency of a company he had believed in and worked in for ten years. He discussed it with his wife (they were married in 1952) and with DeVos. "Of course they wanted Jay," DeVos explains. "They respected his brainpower. I told him to do what he really wanted to do. The offer was lying there; I couldn't hold him back."

For Jay, it was not an opportunity to reject offhandedly. "I considered it seriously, not frivolously," he says. "My basic instincts told me not to do it, but I wanted to make the decision in an intelligent manner. It seemed to be a step up at the time, I suppose, and I think I could have hoped eventually to take over that business. But I knew it was a decision that would be a once-and-for-all thing. I guess in the end it just came down to the fact that I didn't want to break up the partnership with Rich."

So he didn't. He turned down the offer, and returned to Grand Rapids to go back to work. Nutrilite was still in trouble, but the DeVos-Van Andel team was intact.

With the advantages of hindsight, it is possible to look back and see that what is now the Amway Corporation gradually evolved out of the DeVos-Van Andel Nutrilite distributorship during that year from the summer of 1958 to the summer of '59.

The sales organization developed by the Grand Rapids partners (called Ja-Ri Corporation, for obvious reasons) was still strong, despite the internal squabbling at Nutrilite in California. In the fall of 1958, its distributors had organized themselves into an organization they called the American Way Association, in order to provide some cohesion to weather the storm that was building in the Nutrilite leadership. This association had a board (including Van Andel, DeVos, and elected members of the distributor force) to provide the distributors in the Ja-

Ri Corporation with a means of input into management-level decisions. As these developments occurred, the Ja-Ri Corporation's sense of independence from Nutrilite increased.

DeVos and Van Andel decided that the Nutrilite situation was too precarious to depend on. Nutrilite or no Nutrilite, they had a group of distributors to whom they felt responsible, many of whom had left their jobs to go full time. If Nutrilite couldn't provide the leadership to keep those distributors healthy, then it was the responsibility of Van Andel and DeVos to move into that vacuum and lead the way. In the summer of 1958, at a meeting of their leading distributors in Charlevoix, Michigan, they made their announcement: We intend to develop our own product line. We will continue to sell Nutrilite products [they explained] but we can no longer depend solely on that company to supply our distributorships with marketable products. It is up to us to make our own way.

With that explanation, the two partners gave the people there the opportunity to stay with them and the American Way Association, or to remain entirely with Nutrilite. To a person, the leaders at Charlevoix chose to head into new territory with DeVos and Van Andel.

That was the cutting of the umbilical cord which tied the small group to Nutrilite exclusively. A few months later, in early 1959, DeVos and Van Andel sat in the basement office of Jay's home in Ada, Michigan, and officially organized Amway Corporation. It was a bold, hopeful beginning—a gamble that they could make it alone, and go on to build an organization of size and permanence. With the beautiful blessing of hindsight, one can easily see that it would be the start of something big. At the time, one couldn't be so sure.

3 The American Way

It is one thing to adopt a name, switch on the lights, hang a sign on the wall, and bravely throw the doors open for business, and quite another thing altogether to put money in the cash register. Many a little boy has brashly set out to roam the world after breakfast, only to come home, humbled and hungry, at dinner time. The challenge, in business as in life, is not to begin bravely, but to persist and to prosper. Thousands of new businesses start and fail each year. The premium in business is not on fancy proclamations in the morning, but the quiet statements of profit and loss at the end of the day.

Ten years earlier, in the autumn of 1948, when DeVos and Van Andel had just begun their aviation business, both were still attending Calvin College. Over the

Christmas vacation they had gone to Florida together, and there, churning with ideas and eagerness to pour their full effort into the business, they made the decision to leave school and work full time.

Recounting that time, DeVos described their feelings when that decision was made: "We reached the point of saying, Let's quit talking about it and *do* it! Let's get on with it! Let's just *charge!*"

Now, once again, they had crossed the Rubicon. And *charge* they did!

Their biggest challenge at the outset was to develop a product line. They had experimented with a few household items, and believed that the best products to market through a direct sales organization like theirs were everyday commodities—soaps, detergents, household, and personal-care products. In the next few years, they tested that notion with the occasional introduction of big-ticket items into the product line, such as mechanical water softeners and even fall-out shelters, and always returned to their original view that home-care products were best suited to their marketing system.

A tube of toothpaste is easy to sell. Everyone uses it. It runs out and must be replaced, creating the opportunity for repeat business. And, most importantly, it requires no specialized training to sell. One needs no technical expertise to explain to a customer how to operate a bar of soap. There is no installation-and-maintenance problem with a tube of lipstick. "Why do we sell soap?" DeVos asks in one of his speeches. "Because people *buy* soap!"

From the outset, the Amway concept was one of marketing ordinary household items which anyone could sell. Van Andel explains: "In the direct-sales business, one must decide whether he wants an organization of highly specialized, professional salesmen, or a situation in which almost anyone can develop the business and make a profit. We opted for the latter approach. We wanted to provide an opportunity that virtually any hard-working person could take advantage of. With household products, the new distributor doesn't have the task of creating a demand for the product, of convincing the customer that he needs it. The demand is already there. All the distributor must do is say, 'Look, you're buying this product at the supermarket already. I want to offer you a product as good or better at a comparable price, and I'll bring it to your door, give you individual service, and guarantee your money back if you're not satisfied.' Now that's not a bad deal. That is the kind of sales that anyone can do. Household products fit into our concept of a sort of 'Everyman' business, as opposed to a business for big-ticket, supersalesman types."

The first product to be sold in volume by the new company was a liquid all-purpose cleanser called *Frisk*. It was made by a very small manufacturer in Trenton, Michigan, and recommended to Van Andel and DeVos by one of their distributors. It was an unusually effective cleaning liquid, and became the first product on the Amway list, sold in a plastic blue-and-white bottle. A successor to that product still is a staple of the product line, now bearing the name *L.O.C.* (for "liquid organic concentrate"). A Detroit manufacturer named Atco was contracted to provide oven cleaner and furniture polish, and soon after began furnishing a dry-compound laundry detergent called *SA8*. This product also became a popular favorite, and is also near the top of the list in sales volume among Amway products today.

As the Amway product line increased, DeVos and Van

Andel would eventually buy out their suppliers and bring the manufacturing process to Grand Rapids. They had learned from the Nutrilite experience that separate control of the manufacturing and distribution arms of a company is a potentially disastrous situation, and determined to make their own products as soon as possible.

Meanwhile, the growth of the distributor force continued. DeVos and Van Andel had bought a piece of property on a hill overlooking the Thornapple River in a community called Ada, and built homes near one another on that hill. The new Amway Corporation began operating in those houses, with the basements being made into offices. At first the team consisted only of the two men and their wives (Rich was married in 1953), with office help being added as the operation grew.

And grow it did, like a weed in a fertilizer field. DeVos and Van Andel were committed to starting their own company without disrupting the Nutrilite business which they were leaving. As a safeguard against the accusation that they were seducing other Nutrilite distributors away into their fold, they imposed a strict ban on sponsoring Nutrilite distributors. Only their own organization was included in the original Amway group. But the proselytizing of distributors from other companies, even if DeVos and Van Andel had been so inclined, proved not to be necessary. The patented DeVos-Van Andel magic still was a potent force. They worked as if their lives depended on it. Sponsor. Train. Motivate. It has always been the same formula. In the early days Van Andel did most of the sponsoring of new distributors, and DeVos directed the sales force as it was built. They would go into a town—

anywhere within a few hundred miles of Ada—place ads in the paper, make contact with prospects in their homes, and then hold a meeting in a motel room or a rented hall of some sort, and sponsor new distributors.

A trim, thirty-eight-year-old Amway distributor in Detroit remembers those days from an unusual perspective. Wally Buttrick was seventeen years old and made extra money mowing lawns in Ada. He was an ambitious kid, and went around the community knocking on doors, asking for business. One day he knocked on the door of a house on Windy Hill, and Jay Van Andel answered. Buttrick began mowing the Van Andel lawn for one dollar an hour. He remembers that there was a split-rail fence with lots of trimming to do—not an easy yard, he thought. Before long he began working there two days a week, weeding the garden as well as mowing the lawn. He was curious about the office operation that was going on so furiously inside, and when he inquired about it, Van Andel offered him a job, running the mimeograph machine and putting addresses on envelopes. He helped assemble the first eighteen-page career manual, collating the pages on the basement Ping-Pong table.

"Jay was amazing," he says. "He would write all this stuff, then go to the typewriter and type it himself, then run it off on the mimeograph machine, then help put it together and staple it. He was a one-man army." And while Van Andel was doing that, DeVos was running the sales operation. If someone came to Ada to pick up an order, he would go to the basement office, check the order, jump in his car and drive to the warehouse they had rented nearby, fill the order, and put it in the fellow's car for him.

The fledgling Amway operation necessarily involved Betty Van Andel and Helen DeVos. Both wives had the task of maintaining a normal home life for young children, while their husbands conducted the bustling distributor activity literally under their feet. The key roles the two wives played set a pattern that continues in Amway today of husbands and wives working together as a team. Though corporate statistics show that 25 per cent of new distributors are unmarried, the business has a decidedly couples-oriented flavor that encourages men and their wives to build it together.

After a year they moved out of the basement office. They bought an old gas station, forty by sixty feet, in Ada and put their first office and a small print shop there. It was the first of more than seventy-five building projects that would occur from 1960 to 1980. A chart showing the expansion of the physical plant is an impressive indication of the explosive growth the company was experiencing. Two months after moving into the old gas station, a 5,600-square-foot manufacturing facility was added. The next year another 4,000 square feet were added. In 1962 there were six new building projects. The next year a tank farm was added, plus a warehouse, a servicing area for the truck fleet, and the office and manufacturing space was enlarged three times. In 1964 came three more warehouses, a cluster of storage silos, a 20,000-square-foot administration building, and five other expansion projects. And on and on. Explosive growth each year. A railroad spur was added as years passed, and two hangars at the Kent County Airport, and other buildings of almost every description.

The present Amway facility occupies a three-hundred-acre tract, with over one million square feet under roof at Ada, with another half-million square feet in seven Regional Distribution Centers around the country—all from that forty-by-sixty-foot building in 1960!

Those buildings weren't being built just to keep the construction industry healthy. The expansion was forced by a soaring sales volume, which was in turn produced by the growing distributor force. "Those guys worked hard," an Ada resident says. "Every night you could go by there and see the lights on 'til 2:00 or 3:00 A.M." Buttrick graduated from errand-boy status to assisting DeVos on the road. "We started going to places too far away to drive, so they rented a used single-engine plane from a guy who owned a dry-cleaning shop. Later they got a twin-engine Piper, then a Beechcraft. We went all over the country in that thing. It was lots of work, but things were growing so we had fun too."

Why such phenomenal growth? There is no easy answer to that question, but phenomenal it was. From an estimated retail sales volume of half-a-million dollars in 1960, the figure had reached $100 million in 1970, and would pass the $1 billion mark in 1980.

The meteoric development of Amway from that half-million-dollar beginning to its present size ranks among the most impressive such success stories in recent corporate history. It is another bit of evidence that the classic "American Dream" is still a possible dream, one that can still come true. The storybook quality of the DeVos-Van Andel rise to prominence includes a fitting final footnote: in 1972, less than two dozen years after the two young partners had become Nutrilite distributors, Amway bought controlling interest in Nutrilite, Inc., and

27

merged it into their company. Van Andel and DeVos had always believed strongly in the quality of Nutrilite food supplements (each has personally never stopped using the products), and took advantage of an opportunity to buy control of the company when it occurred.

Since that time the food-supplement company, complete with its California farms and manufacturing facilities, has been a part of the Amway operation, and all its products are offered to customers as part of the Amway product list. Events have come full circle since 1949, and today DeVos and Van Andel are once again with Nutrilite—as president and chairman of the board, respectively.

There have been many factors which have spurred Amway's growth, but the heart of the company's tremendous vitality may have been an attitude, more than the marketing plan or the economic climate. A friend recalls driving past the Amway plant late one night in the early 1960s. It was a chilly night, about 11:30 P.M., and he was surprised to see Rich DeVos and Jay Van Andel there on the front lawn, digging a hole in which to erect a sign that lay nearby. "What in the world are you fellows doing *that* for?" he asked incredulously. They paused in their digging. One of them looked up at him, grinned, and said, "Well, what's the use in paying somebody else to do something you can do yourself?"

4 The Plan

What is an Amway distributor, and what does one do?

Basically, Amway distributors do two things: They sell Amway products to their friends, neighbors, and other retail customers—and they recruit other people to do the same.

Selling the products is simple. The distributor has a product list of about 300 items to offer the customer. These products are made by Amway, usually come in concentrated form, and most are everyday items for home and personal care that everyone uses. The distributor makes an immediate income on all the products he sells, usually about 30 percent of the retail price.

The second activity—that of recruiting other people to become distributors—is called "sponsoring." Under some conditions, the distributor may receive a bonus on the sales volume of anyone he brings into the business. There is no money to be made merely for recruiting a new distributor, but if that distributor actually goes to work and generates sales, the company pays a bonus to the sponsor for supplying him with products and training him in sales techniques. One can make a potentially large income if there are large numbers of people working actively in the Amway business whom he or she has sponsored.

So successful Amway distributors are constantly working not only to sell products themselves, but to urge other people to "go thou and do likewise." Amway operates a string of warehouses around the country called Regional Distribution Centers, and products are shipped from these points to the distributors, who take them personally to the customer. It is strictly a cash-as-you-go proposition; the customer pays cash to the distributor, and the distributor pays cash to the company.

The world of Amway has its own vocabulary, parts of which are as understandable as Chinese to someone not privy to the jargon. For the uninitiated reader, here is a quick and handy Amway glossary:

Sponsor To "sponsor" another individual is to bring him into the business, by persuading him to sign an application and become a distributor himself. Mr. *A* receives no money for sponsoring Mr. *B*, but agrees to train, supply, and motivate him, and receives a bonus from the corporation based on Mr. *B*'s sales volume, as Mr. *B* actually develops the business.

Leg Every new distributor whom Mr. *A* sponsors becomes a "leg" in his organization. When Mr. *A* sponsors Mr. *B*, Mr. *B* is one of his legs, along with anyone whom Mr. *B* might ultimately sponsor. So the number of legs Mr. *A* has is the same as the number of people he has personally sponsored. (Note: Mr. *A* might as easily be called *Mrs. A*, as many women are successful distributors.)

Personal group All the distributors whom Mr. *A* has sponsored, plus those whom *they* have sponsored, and so on, up to the first Direct Distributor. To say that Mr. *X* is in Mr. *A*'s "personal group" doesn't mean that Mr. *A* is his boss, or any such thing as that. It simply means that Mr. *X* is somewhere in the "family tree."

Direct Distributor Becoming a Direct Distributor is the first major goal in the Amway business. That level is reached when a distributor and his or her group generate sales of approximately $8,000 per month for three straight months. (The exact dollar amount changes as it is periodically adjusted for inflation.) When Mr. *A* becomes a Direct Distributor, he purchases his products directly from the corporation, rather than from his sponsor.

Show the plan To "show the plan" is to explain the Amway sales and marketing plan to a prospect. Mr. *A* may show the plan with the use of a blackboard, slides, flip chart, or simply by telling the prospect how the system works.

Sponsoring meeting Any meeting in which a distributor brings a number of prospects together to show the plan to all of them simultaneously.

Break off a Direct When Mr. *A* sponsors Mr. *B* into the business, and Mr. *B* reaches the level of a Direct Distributor, Mr. *A* is said to have "broken off a direct Distributor." In other words, he has helped a distributor whom he sponsored to reach the level of Direct Distributor. The corporation pays a monthly bonus to Mr. *A* for every person he breaks off, based on a 3 per cent of the new Direct's volume.

Pin awards Amway has a series of pins which are awarded to Direct Distributors who continue to increase their businesses. These pins indicate roughly how big Mr. *A*'s volume has become, and the size of his income. The pin awards, in ascending order, are as follows: RUBY, PEARL, EMERALD, DIAMOND, DOUBLE DIAMOND, TRIPLE DIAMOND, CROWN, CROWN AMBASSADOR.

It is virtually impossible to fix a dollar amount on the incomes of distributors at these levels, but one must surmise, in observing their lifestyles, that the income for "Diamonds" or above is very good indeed. The level of "Crown" has been reached by about two dozen distributorships. The first Crown couple were Charlie and Elsie Marsh, a New York couple, whose story was one of the first—and still is one of the best—examples of the classic Amway success story. The Marshes came into Amway in 1964, and in 1970 achieved the Crown level. "They showed it could be done," one Amway official said. "No matter how many Crowns there are in the future, Charlie and Elsie will always be the ones who showed the way."

The Amway system seems to attract ambitious husband-wife teams like the Marshes, and the pin awards are there to give them a tangible mountain to climb.

Amway Corporation today is a far cry from the small, bustling operation of 1960. Growth has continued unabated since the inception of the company, and last fiscal year saw the corporation's greatest increase in its history. Consolidated revenues last year exceeded 1 billion dollars— or an estimated retail volume of 1.4 billion dollars. There are over 700,000 U.S. active distributorships in the business today, and at least 75 per cent are couples, placing the total number of Amway "people" somewhere over 1 million.

The company holds dozens of conventions and rallies each year, ranging in size from very small meetings to the 30,000-plus who attended a Washington, D.C., rally in 1975. Each fall, the company celebrates Free Enterprise Day, with an estimated 300,000 people attending 300 simultaneous rallies across the country.

The home office operation at Ada is sleek and sophisticated. In 1973 the new Center for Free Enterprise was dedicated in Ada by then-Congressman Gerald R. Ford and Governor William G. Milliken of Michigan. It now includes the executive office area, plus displays explaining the free-enterprise system, an auditorium, an Amway Museum, and portrait sculptures of the founders, which were placed there by the distributors themselves. The Ada facility employs 6,000 people. That number includes, in addition to plant employees, chemists and scientists in the research and development laboratories; computer experts to run the computers and other high-speed processing equipment; a staff of attorneys;

printers to operate the four huge presses in the printing plant; artists and photographers in the graphic-arts studio; and many other persons with specialized skills. Amway makes its own cardboard boxes and plastic bottles, shoots its own commercial photography, and prints its own containers, labels, and sales material.

A fleet of trucks (fifty tractor-trailer rigs) hauls products to the regional warehouses, aided by red-white-and-blue Amway railway cars. The aviation department employs a staff of pilots and mechanics to operate the company's two BAC 1–11 jets and three smaller Cessna jets and a helicopter. The two larger planes are similar, with plush custom-made interiors. Each carries 25 passengers and a crew of 3, flies 450 miles per hour at an altitude of 39,000 feet, and travels an average of 400,000 miles per year, taking Amway executives and distributors around the country. And there is the corporate diesel yacht, the *Enterprise III,* 131-foot vessel that sleeps ten guests (plus crew) and serves as a "floating conference center" in the Caribbean for top-performing distributors.

All the facilities, hardware, and staff of the Amway home office in Ada have the task of helping the distributors in the field build stronger, more profitable businesses. What is good for the distributors is good for Amway. Amway products are not sold in supermarkets or drugstores, and the corporation therefore depends on the distributor force to market everything it produces. It is a good arrangement, because it demands that corporate leaders work constantly to help the distributor be more productive. "The corporation at Ada is the heart of Amway, but we are the blood," one distributor described it.

To keep that "blood" pumping, the company maintains a large number of services to help distributors build their businesses. An audiovisual department produces cassette tapes and 16-mm films explaining the Amway opportunity. A virtual flood of printed material is mailed—over several million copies of the monthly magazine *Amagram* go out per year, and other materials are printed in English, Spanish, French, German, and Chinese. Contact with the distributor force is also maintained by the work of a Travel Team, an aggressive group of young men with an appetite for the road who conduct some 150 rallies and seminars around the country each year. The corporation also has a limited program of consumer advertising in the national media: ads in magazines such as *Time, People,* and *Ebony;* television spots on the major television networks; and Paul Harvey's radio-news show.

The company provides other services to the distributor force which are not directly related to the business itself. An example is the Amway Mutual Fund, which is a professionally managed investment company in which many distributors have invested. Through their membership in the Amway Distributors Association, they can also participate in group medical insurance programs. Amway Corporation purchased the Mutual Broadcasting System, the nation's largest radio network, in 1978.

Amway Corporation has become a big, sleek, and well-oiled piece of commercial machinery—so much that at times its greatest danger seems to be that of growing too big to maintain the personal touch that has made it such a phenomenal success. Its amazing growth can continue only so long as its leaders keep distributors at the center of it all. Will bigness and success rob Amway of that personal touch on which the business thrives?

"No way," says Bill Britt, a North Carolina distributor who wears a Triple Diamond pin. "Absolutely no way that will happen. We have a couple of guys up there in Ada who have been where we are, and they won't ever let this company lose the personal flavor it has now. Rich and Jay built it just like we're doing, and I built it just like my newest distributor is doing, and so on. In this business, waking up the potential in another person is just like striking a match. Once you've had the thrill of doing that for people, you don't forget it."

5 A Matter of Trust

There is a sentence, discreetly tucked away in the official "fact sheet" published by Amway, that describes the ownership of the company. "Amway Corporation," it states succinctly, "is privately held by the DeVos and Van Andel families."

Privately held. That means they own it outright, with no platoons of hungry stockholders to influence their judgments. *Forbes,* the well-known national business magazine, recently ranked Amway as among the largest such "privately held" companies in the United States. This makes for an unusual situation in top corporate management. Sole ownership has allowed the two owners to operate the company without being subject to the internal policies of a publicly held corporation. DeVos is "president" and Van Andel is "chairman of the board" simply because that is a convenient way to describe their joint leadership of the company.

For several years, when Amway was small, the men assumed those two titles alternately. One would be president and the other would be chairman for a year, then they would switch. That became an awkward way of doing things, and one day DeVos said to his partner, "Look, Jay, you're older than I am—why don't you go ahead and be chairman of the board." In that informal way the permanent titles were fixed.

Such informality characterizes the way Van Andel and DeVos have always made policy at Amway. They know one another well enough that they are able to mesh their two distinct styles with a minimum of friction. "We just chew on things, and finally somebody will say, 'Well, let's do it this way,'" DeVos explains.

Van Andel adds to that, "We have a standing rule that if one of us objects to something, we don't do it. Period. That applies to all decisions, large or small. We also do not disagree with each other in the presence of other people. We have developed some pretty good signals between ourselves, to let the other know to back off until we can talk it over privately."

There are five executive vice-presidents at Amway who direct the functions of the company. All report directly to Van Andel and DeVos, and together they make up a Management Committee which is empowered to respond to any emergency which arises in the absence of the two leaders. This team of executives, as well as other management officials, has been assembled in an informal way that fits Amway's overall corporate style.

Almost none of the higher-ranking Amway officials have come from the distributor forces. The most notable exception to this rule, Roger Krause, was brought into the Ada office after building a Crown Direct distributorship with his parents. A few other Amway officers have had brief experiences as distributors, but Amway generally regards that as an undesirable practice. Amway, like any other large corporation, has become a bureaucracy of sorts, and the record shows that good entrepreneurs rarely make happy bureaucrats.

Management recruiting has occurred in a variety of ways. Krause came from the field. Bill Hemmer was referred by an employment agency. Wally Buttrick began by mowing Van Andel's lawn, went on to become a regional sales coordinator, then resigned his job to become a distributor—an ironic reversal of the Krause pattern. Randy Preston, now a vice-president, was offered a job when he met DeVos at a PTA meeting. He heard DeVos speak that night, went up afterwards to introduce himself, and soon after became personnel director of what was then a small company.

With this unique management system, the partners have assembled an effective supporting cast. A key member of the team almost since the beginning has been Bill Halliday, an attorney, has been chief legal advisor to DeVos and Van Andel for twenty-five years. He spent World War II in the Pacific, interrogating Japanese prisoners of war and translating for the First Cavalry (he still speaks Japanese "a little"), and later served as Trial Counsel for general courtmartial cases in Judge Advocate General Corps.

Halliday met Devos and Van Andel in 1951, when they asked him to collect a bad debt for them. He succeeeded, and did occasional legal work for them, and they became good friends. It was Halliday who wrote the papers of incorporation for Amway in 1959. In 1966 he came aboard as a full-time corporate attorney, and now supervises the legal staff and other departments. He has perhaps watched DeVos and Van Andel closely over a longer period of time than anyone else, and his respect for them is complete.

"There is no doubt in my mind," he says, "that it is the synergistic effect of those two guys that has made Amway what it is."

Has he ever heard them fight? "Well, sure," he replies. "When something new comes along, they may be very fixed at opposite poles. They'll raise their voices and argue just like any other two strong-willed, bright, stubborn people. But each gives and they finally meet, usually in the middle. It's great for two guys to be able to work that way."

As an attorney, Halliday is particularly proud of what he calls the "total integrity of Rich and Jay, and of this company" since he has been acquainted with their operation.

"I know of no one who has ever lost a dime in Amway," he states flatly.

And, indeed, in the sifting of comments and observations from dozens of disparate sources, the theme of scrupulous honesty does emerge. Amway distributors seem eager to tell not only that the company has dealt fairly with them, but that it frequently goes beyond its legal requirements to see that individual distributors are treated fairly. To prevent distributors from having products "dumped" on them, Amway has an automatic buy-back provision, and has honored it even in rather extreme cases. A distributor was killed in an accident several years ago, for example, who had several thousand dollars' worth of products in his garage. Amway bought it all back from his estate.

Such stories abound. One distributor recalls the company buying a new carpet for a customer who didn't read the label and dumped an entire bottle of carpet shampoo on his rug, ruining it. Bob Vest, a Double Diamond says, "There has never been any dramatic incident that convinced me of the integrity of the company, but over the years, every promise has been kept. They have always done what they said they would do, and then some. It's the small things that add up. They have never questioned the return of an item. And occasionally, if I have something missing when my products arrive, and I call and say, 'Hey, I didn't get a case of so-and-so,' there's no problem, no questions asked. They just send it to you."

Apparently most distributors have a similar experience with the company. It could be argued, of course, that distributors who are treated badly are those who have quit the business, and therefore one must talk to them to get a more balanced picture. But conversations with the dropouts reveal a very similar attitude. The typical statement from a former distributor goes something like this: "Amway is all right. They treated me fine. No complaints. It just wasn't for me."

That impression is supported by a survey conducted by the company, in which researchers contacted 250 nonrenewing distributors, 5 in each of 50 states. The reasons offered for quitting the business were in almost every case personal—a new job, a pregnancy, simple loss of interest. When asked how many products they were stuck with, no one had more than one hundred dollars' worth of stock remaining, and 80 per cent of those polled had less then twenty dollars' worth. The final question: Would you like Amway to buy whatever products you have back from you? The response: 249 out of 250 said, "No, thanks. We'd rather keep them than have our money back."

The issue of corporate integrity is a critical one for Amway and other direct-sales companies. They frankly admit to an image problem, arising largely from the so-called pyramid scandals of the early 1970s and a widespread public misunderstanding of the direct-sales business. When Glenn Turner, the self-styled Florida motivational whiz, was indicted a few years ago on fraud charges, the laws against pyramid sales schemes received page one attention. The problem that creates for Amway is the tendency by the public to lump all direct-sales companies into the pyramid category.

Pyramid companies are clearly fraudulent, and are illegal in most states. The Amway system is not a pyramid—that much can be stated unequivocally. In fact, Amway pushed hard for the strict laws against pyramiding which were passed in most states in 1972 and '73. Amway's legal staff has helped draft the legislation banning such operations in several jurisdictions, acting as consultants to legislators and their staffs. Ironic then, that Amway is often confused with the pyramids.

The two major illegal aspects of pyramid schemes are (1) the paying of a so-called headhunter's fee, in which a person is paid to sign another person up, whether he produces anything or not; and (2) the buying of distributorships, either by paying a large sum outright, or by a required purchase of large amounts of inventory. In both cases, Amway's skirts are clean. The Amway system does not pay a sign-up fee, nor does it require the new distributor to buy inventory. As one distributor puts it, "There's no way you can lose anything in Amway except a few hours of your time."

Ironically, many successful distributors have been recruited as a result of their preconceived notion that Amway was in some way fraudulent. A graphic example is Jose Melina, an assistant attorney general in Puerto Rico. He had directed the legal battle against the Glenn Turner pyramid scheme, and when Amway came to the island, began an inquiry into its business practices, thinking it might also be legally vulnerable. He was instead impressed with its soundness, was sponsored, and is now a Direct Distributor. Peter Muller-Meerkatz, a West German grad student, was writing his doctoral thesis on pyramid schemes and answered an Amway ad in the paper to get material for his research. Same story: he saw the plan, got in, and now is Germany's top producer.

Though Amway seems to be gaining ground in separating itself from these get-rich-quick schemes in the public eye, its efforts in that direction have not been helped by the news in April of 1975 that a complaint had been filed against them by the Federal Trade Commission. (The complaint involves such technicalities as Amway's right to prevent its products from being sold in stores.) Though the complaint was filed in the Bureau of Competition—rather than the Bureau of Fraud—and therefore does not allege any illegality or seek any penalties, the complaint does detract from the company's effort to keep a first-class public image.

The FTC has also filed complaints or launched investigations against Sears, Roebuck and Co.; Kellogg Company; Borden Inc.' Revlon Inc.; Whirlpool Corporation; Reynolds Tobacco Co.; Quaker Oats Co.; Inc.; and just about every other American company that has managed to show a profit during the past few years.

On May 24, 1979, the Federal Trade Commission published its Opinion and Final Order in the Amway case. After more than four years of legal proceedings, preceded by six years of investigation involving the review of thousands of documents and interviews with hundreds of distributors, The FTC found that Amway had "injected a vigorous new competitive presence into a highly concentrated market" and upheld the Amway Sales and Marketing Plan.

The FTC also ruled that neither Amway, The Amway Distributors Association, nor Amway distributors can fix prices at which an Amway distributor can sell Amway products. The FTC also directed that, in explaining the marketing plan to prospective distributors, adequate attention must be given to average earnings by Amway distributors.

The final FTC rulings were greeted by Amway people as a welcome affirmation of their respectability in the American marketplace.

6 Chairman of the Board

Analyzing Jay Van Andel is rather like trying to peel an onion. After stripping one layer away, one finds another underneath, and another, and another.

A line from John Steinbeck comes to mind in describing Van Andel—a passage from *The Wayward Bus*, in which Steinbeck describes one of his characters: "... Norma was even more submerged than an iceberg. Only the tiniest part of Norma showed above the surface. For the greatest and best and most beautiful part of Norma lay behind her eyes, sealed and protected."

Ask anyone who has worked with Jay Van Andel, and he will tell you without hesitation that Van Andel is one of the most capable men he knows. It is almost impossible to ask about the man without hearing at length about his intelligence, his ability to digest and assimilate information rapidly, his unerring judgment when important decisions are to be made. And one requires only a little time in conversation with Van Andel himself to confirm those assessments. Those qualities are so self-evident, in fact, that it seems frivolous to describe them at length—rather like dwelling on the fact that Grace Kelly is a beautiful woman, or discussing the fact that King Kong is indeed a *large* animal.

But with Van Andel the greatest and best and most beautiful part—to borrow from Steinbeck—lies beneath that rather imposing surface. Like the onion, he has many layers; and the top one, that fine mind that has served him so well over the years, sometimes glitters so brightly, impresses so thoroughly, that one never pulls it aside to discover the subtler and warmer layers underneath.

Van Andel constantly surprises. Publicly he projects an image of great reserve and austerity; privately it is not the black limousine which he favors, but a sleek, powerful Lamborghini and a custom-built Excalibur classic. He has been called "Mr. Inside" at Amway, a tag which suggests that his technical abilities—and not the more publicly visible motivational skills—are his strong suit. Yet he brought a crowd of eighteen thousand distributors to their feet in a Washington, D.C., convention, not once, but twenty-eight times, as they interrupted his speech with standing applause. ("Jay," an observer remarked on that occasion, "has discovered the microphone.") He skis and swims but usually shuns competitive athletic activity, almost never plays tennis or golf; but he took a friend on a hike one day, climbing up and down the massive sand dunes by the shore of Lake Michigan, and left the friend, many years his junior, panting and pale-faced and far behind. Shades of Theodore Roosevelt.

The surprises are always there, lying just behind whatever easy descriptive or pat summation might be applied to him. There are few easy labels for him.

Van Andel flies an unusual flag over his vacation home in Holland, Michigan. It is the flag of Friesland, an area of the Netherlands which was once an independent state, and from which his mother emigrated around the turn of the century. Van Andel's ties to his Dutch ancestry are strong and deep. His father, whose family emigrated from near Amsterdam, owned and operated an auto agency, and Jay acquired from him and from his grandfathers, a sense of independence, the spirit of the entrepreneur, which would be so important to him in later years.

After high school, he entered Calvin College, where a recruiter persuaded him to enlist in the U.S. Army Air Corps. "He promised me lots of things if I would join," Van Andel explains, "and not being very well schooled in life at that time, I believed him." He enlisted in 1942 as a private and came out four years later as a first lieutenant, which says something about his ability to learn the system and move upward in it. He was sent to Florida for basic training and was barracked in a tent, on what had formerly been a golf course in Saint Petersburg. He remembers "slogging around in the dust and dirt and looking up, seeing the officers sitting in the shade, sipping drinks on the country-club veranda. The thought occurred to me then: 'There must be a way for me to be up there instead of down here.'"

He found the way. He applied for bombsight school, was told he had to place in the top 10 per cent of his group to be accepted for officer training, and made it. The next year may have been the most important year of his life. He was sent to Yale University for a year of officer's training as an air corps cadet in armament and chemical warfare. Even in wartime, even for military training, Yale is Yale. The regimen was tough and Van Andel thrived on it. He was up at 4:00 A.M., lights out at 9:00 P.M., every day, six-and-one-half days a week. "That year changed my whole view of life. I discovered that by gritting my teeth I could do anything. I realized during that year that I could stay up with the best of them, that it was possible to do things I never thought I could do before." Not that it was easy; he recalls many occasions when he sat in the shower rooms—the only place to go after lights-out—to study through the night.

Perhaps it is appropriate that Van Andel met his wife while he was working. His aunt was a Nutrilite customer who was a housekeeper for the Hoekstra family. Jay called on Mrs. Hoekstra one morning in 1951 to sell her Nutrilite, and was met at the door by the blonde daughter of the household, whose name was Betty, and who became his wife the next year.

The conviction that he could "stay up with the best of them" has been confirmed throughout the past twenty-five years in another hotly competitive arena, that of big business. As chairman of the board, he teams with Rich DeVos to oversee Amway's entire corporate activity, and still finds time for a wide range of other responsibilities. He is chairman of the board of the United States Chamber of Commerce; is board chairman of the Soap and Detergent Association of the U.S.A.; is a trustee of Hillsdale College; and sits on at least two dozen other assorted boards and councils. His awards and honors, *Who's Who* listings, and other credits take several pages merely to list.

Politics occupies much of Van Andel's time. He is active in the Republican Party, serves as state finance chairman for the party, and is board chairman of Citizen's Choice. A longstanding friendship with Gerald R. Ford brought both Van Andel and DeVos more closely into the action of national politics during the Ford presidency, and Van Andel and his wife, Betty, have been frequent guests at the White House. Van Andel and DeVos bought half-page ads in major Michigan newspapers during the 1976 primary campaign urging their friends to support Ford's bid for renomination.

Van Andel, who has received an honorary doctorate from Northern Michigan University, is a man of refined intellectual interests. He is something of a Shakespeare buff, and with his wife makes a regular yearly trek to Stratford, Ontario, to attend the Shakespeare festival there. One year recently he saw two full-length plays (*Hamlet* and *Antony and Cleopatra*) back-to-back, and admitted that, even for him, that was too much Shakespeare for one day! Though he once intended to become an aeronautical engineer, his interests now seem to run in philosophical and literary directions. His reading often includes history and biographies, especially political biographies. (Interestingly, this quintessential Republican, when asked to name two political books he has read recently, named biographies of two Democrats, Presidents Lyndon Johnson and Harry S. Truman.)

Life is not all books and business for Van Andel. His hobbies include organic gardening (he grows orchids and tropical fruit in a greenhouse) and collecting sculpture and paintings from various points in his far-flung travels.

Though he is now, by any yardstick, a very wealthy man, Van Andel scoffs at the idea that the good life may have taken the sharp edge off his competitive drive. "Not at all!" he declares. "Sitting around doing nothing is not my idea of an enjoyable existence. We've just begun to accomplish all that we can with Amway."

But now that you have arrived, doesn't it all become a little less exciting? "Well, I might agree that the journey is more interesting than the destination. But we're still making the journey. If personal wealth were our prime goal, then one could say that we have arrived. But there are more important goals. The greatest thrill to us is seeing the Amway business opportunity improve the lives of people all over the world. That is an unending challenge."

Jay Van Andel is somewhat more subdued, somewhat more private a person than his partner. He enjoys spending time with Betty and their four children—Nan, Steve, Dave, and Barbara—and with a small group of close friends, many of them also successful entrepreneurs, whom he sees socially. But one must remember that the surprises are there, always forcing a re-definition of Van Andel whenever a cliche seems about to catch up with him. For all his reserve, he seems willing to show to those who look for it a warmth that is personal and genuine. Distributors in the Amway world—even those who have never known him personally—somehow sense this warmth, and the great respect, bordering on awe, with which they regard him is mingled with an equal amount of affection.

To hundreds of thousands of Amway distributors, Jay

Van Andel is the Rock of Gibraltar.

"I personally have never been the kind of individual to be shocked by reversals of any kind," Van Andel mused one day. "I have never been one to react by falling apart, by saying, 'Oh, my, what are we going to do?' People like that are usually failures, in business or anything else. I have always tried to react to any sort of problem by saying, 'Well, how do we fix it? Where do we go from here?' And I think that is a valuable posture toward life. If the wheels fall off, just put them back on again. No need to get excited. No point in getting emotional about it. Just put them back on again and keep going."

That attitude, that posture toward life, is something one can't see on the surface of a man. It is one of those submerged qualities, one of those "greatest and best and most beautiful parts" that lie beneath the surface of Jay Van Andel.

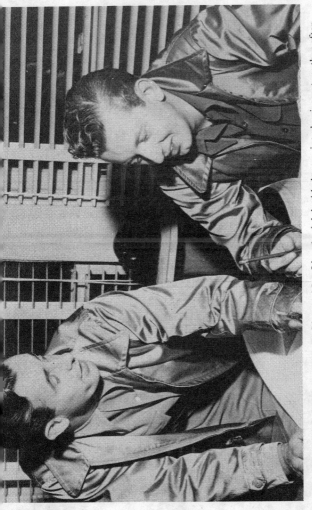

High-school buddies Rich DeVos and Jay Van Andel decided to go into business together after World War II. They formed a partnership in a flying school and air charter business from 1945 through 1948.

Amway's first business office. It was located in the basement of Jay Van Andel's home. Kay Evans (left) continued with the company as executive assistant to the president and chairman of the board until her retirement in January 1976.

Amway's first warehouse was located in the former post office building in Ada, Michigan.

1960-61 Amway Distributors Association Board of Directors: seated left to right are Les Chapin, Wes Hursh, Evangeline Krause, Jere Dutt, Jay Van Andel, Walter Bass, Rich DeVos, Eleanor Teitsma, Joe Victor, Roland Diehl, Fred Hansen. Standing are Neil Maaskant and William Nichols.

In 1962 an executive office building was completed.

A subsidiary of Amway Corporation since 1972, Nutrilite Products, Inc., is headquartered in Buena Park, California.

The Amway Corporation Headquarters/Administration/Manufacturing/Distribution complex now covers in excess of one million square feet and is located on a 300-acre site along the Grand River in Ada.

Among those present at the dedication ceremonies for the Center of Free Enterprise were Gerald R. Ford, William Milliken, Helen DeVos, Richard M. DeVos, Rev. Billy Zeoli, Jay Van Andel and Betty Van Andel. The date was May 25, 1973.

This handsome building is the completed Center of Free Enterprise.

Amway's first Double Diamond Direct Distributors, Jere and Eileen Dutt of Ohio, welcomed on their "day at Ada" in 1966 by Jay Van Andel and Rich DeVos.

Amway's fully automated liquid manufacturing line. Flow begins at upper left, where bottles are molded from plastic beads, and ends at lower right, where filled and labeled bottles packed in cases exit to the warehouse.

Rich and Helen DeVos smile for an eager photographer at an award banquet.

7 The President

Richard M. DeVos plays pretty good tennis. He is left-handed, and his serve is a deep, slicing ball that keeps twisting away from his opponent, making it deceptively hard to return. When the opponent does succeed in getting the ball back up to the net, DeVos is usually waiting there to hammer it past him for the point.

He does other things well, too.

DeVos is a fit and tanned fifty-five-year-old who has that personal magnetism that has come to be called *charisma*. It is difficult to define, this quality that draws people to him, but clearly it is there. He walks into a room, and soon people are clustering around him. Well-tailored suit. Loose, easy approach. He stands so erect-ly that he sometimes bends slightly backward from the waist. Muted wire-rim glasses. He speaks easily, confidently, in short, quick bursts of words. Rich DeVos looks and talks and moves like a winner.

And well he should. For the last thirty years, he has been winning at virtually everything he tries, and that includes some challenges far more momentous than an afternoon tennis match. As the president of Amway Corporation, he sits atop a large personal fortune, and people who have heard the story of his almost-miraculous rise from a modest workingman's home to wealth and leadership in the business world are tempted to think of him purely in terms of his business success. There is a common stereotype of the obsessive hard-driving business tycoon whose only talent is for making money. However one may shove and squeeze, it is simply impossible to put DeVos into that mold. He is far too multidimensional to be so easily categorized.

The DeVos reputation as a public speaker is well known. He has won many awards for his speaking, and the demand for his presence on the speaker's platform is great. His speaking style is informal and relaxed, but he is capable—sometimes at unexpected moments—of sudden, moving intensity. He does not bludgeon a crowd, but beguiles it, scoring his points deftly as he goes. He fights with a rapier, rather than a broadsword, and when he is finished he almost always has worked his will with the audience. When he is right, there is no one anywhere who is better. DeVos debated occasionally in high school (one typical issue was "Resolved: That it is better to live in the city than in the country"), and took a public-speaking course in Grand Rapids as a young businessman. But no one who hears him doubts that today he operates onstage by instinct. He knows those people out there; somehow he is able to identify with what they think, how they feel. He cajoles, he roars, he reasons calmly, he exhorts—in short, he *communicates* with the audience, and usually, in the words of the Green Bay *Gazette*, he "moves from one standing ovation to another."

DeVos speaks frequently to Amway audiences, but probably is more often found on other platforms. In the course of a single assignment, one writer trailing DeVos heard him speak at a high-school commencement, a community patriotic rally, a convention of school superintendents, a Boy Scout rally, and a meeting of church leaders in his denomination. He was good every time.

DeVos authored a book entitled *Believe!* in 1975, weaving sections from some of his speeches with other material in a statement of his personal creed. In the book, he discusses his point of view on subjects such as Americanism, free enterprise, religion, the family. The Fleming H. Revell Company, a New Jersey publisher, urged DeVos for two years to write a book, and when he finally agreed, their expectations proved well founded. *Believe!* has sold over 500,000 copies in hardcover and paperback editions (Pocket Books), and made several best-seller lists around the country. In the Walden Books chain—the nation's largest—it was the number one nonfiction best-seller for six consecutive weeks. One newspaper reviewer predicted it "will become a classic in self-improvement books."

Self-improvement is a subject on which DeVos can speak with some authority. He grew up in Grand Rapids in a day when "you got a penny on Saturday morning and you could spend it any way you liked." Born in 1926, he was a true product of the depression years. As a child, he lived upstairs in his grandfather's home, and remembers selling leftover vegetables door-to-door for extra pocket change. "I peddled newspapers, worked in a gas station, that sort of thing. No big deal. Everybody did it. We may have been poor, but we certainly had no sense of being put down. We were no poorer than anybody else in those days." One gets the impression today that he feels too much is made of that early deprivation, and he probably is right. The tendency is to lean too heavily on the rags-to-riches formula, and to make the rags more ragged than they really were. DeVos grew up in a fairly typical depression-era home, and it is only in retrospect that it seems worse than that.

In high school he made "decent grades, I guess. I'm sure they weren't spectacular." Already emerging as a leader, he was elected president of his class at Christian High School. Upon graduation, he enlisted in the air force; was sent to a school for glider mechanics in Texas; then to the Carolinas ("I did nothing but coil rope all day long. Exciting job."); and finally was shipped to the Pacific as part of the buildup before the expected invasion of Japan. He was on his way to the Pacific when the bomb was dropped on Hiroshima, and by the time he reached the island of Tinian, the war was over. Tinian was a B-29 base, and he spent the rest of his military hitch there, driving a truck.

Those war years—teenage years for DeVos—made a permanent mark on him. As most men of his generation do, he remembers hearing about Pearl Harbor, and the wartime speeches of FDR. Those years put in him a deep, permanent love for his country, an emotional attachment, that still fuels his powerful sense of patriotism. "I think most men my age feel that way." DeVos shrugs. "We came up tough. We went off to fight for what we had, what we loved. We knew who the enemy was. And that makes a guy appreciate his country and want to stand up for it."

That love for America has always been a high priority for DeVos, and for the Amway company itself. His most famous speech is called "Selling America" (the text of the speech so impressed Congressman Gerald R. Ford that he read it into the *Congressional Record* in 1965). He has received many awards for his efforts to remind people of the values of the American system. That work, along with his management genius and business leadership, has brought two honorary degrees his way. In 1976 he received the honorary Doctor of Laws degree from Oral Roberts University (in Tulsa, Oklahoma) and from Grove City College (in Pennsylvania). It has placed him on the board of the prestigious National Association of Manufacturers and a whole string of other boards (a bank, a state college, The United Way, and so on), and placed his name on a long list of *Who's Who* publications.

DeVos met his wife, Helen, when she was a student at Calvin College, where he attended briefly. Her father was the deputy superintendent of Kent County (Michigan) schools, and her interest in music and art has likely influenced the attention her husband gives to those areas. She is an officer on the board of directors of the Grand Rapids Symphony, and has taken an interest in the city's cultural life for years. The DeVoses are reluctant to discuss their private philanthropy, but occasionally news of a particular gift surfaces in the local newspapers. It was reported recently that they have made a forty-thousand-dollar annual gift to endow a string quartet for promising young musicians in the symphony. The members of the group asked to be called the DeVos String Quartet, and today they bear that name. They were selected as the state Quartet-in-Residence for Michigan for the 1976-77 concert season, and have been favorably received (a review of a recent concert: "... brilliant display of timing and teamwork ... truly a masterpiece") whenever they have performed.

DeVos is not himself a musician, but he recently was tapped to narrate the *Lincoln Portrait*, a familiar Aaron Copland work, in a performance by the Grand Rapids Symphony. The papers the next day called the DeVos performance "dramatic," "poignant," and said his rendition "left goose bumps on the audience."

It is impossible in describing DeVos to ignore the fact of his personal wealth. Particularly to those who have very little of it, few things are more interesting than money, and DeVos obviously has plenty of it. How much? He won't say. Maybe he doesn't even know. One certainly gets the impression that he doesn't spend much time counting it.

When did he make his first million, or first realize he was a millionaire? "I honestly don't have any idea," he replies. "Making a million dollars just wasn't a milestone to us. We weren't interested in being called 'millionaires'; we were just interested in building a big business. Reaching a million wasn't that big a deal to Jay or me either. I think maybe I didn't realize we were worth a million until somebody offered us twenty million for the business."

Rich DeVos obviously didn't achieve all that he has achieved without a razor-sharp mind and a hard edge beneath that relaxed surface. For all his warmth and generosity, he does not suffer fools gladly. He can be direct—even blunt—when he feels the situation calls for it. People who worked with him in the old days remember that the DeVos temper had a shorter fuse then, that he wasted no words when he chose to bring the troops into line. "He was never unkind," one staff member says, "but he could really lay it on the line. He expected a lot, and when people didn't deliver, he could lay them open without flinching."

But did you like him?

"We loved him like a brother."

And for those who have known DeVos well, that seems always to be the bottom line. For all his talent and energy—those typical traits of a successful executive—the characteristic that seems to draw people to DeVos is that he has a soft spot—a streak of love or sentimentality or something—and from time to time it shows. It shows in the eloquent simplicity of the dedication of his book: "To my wife, Helen, and our children, Dick, Dan, Cheri, Doug, whom I love very much." No gilding. No wasted words. Straightforward and unadorned. It shows on occasions like the dedication of the Center for Free Enterprise, when he wept openly before the future president of the United States and thousands in the gathered crowd. It shows when he sits in an audience at Diamond Club and listens to new members tell their stories, soaking up the words with the contented look of a man warming himself before a fireplace on a cold night.

Rich DeVos has the toughness, the resilience, the hard-nosed business pragmatism to build a business like Amway—and a wide streak of old-fashioned love and concern that gives human meaning to what he has done.

8 Westboro, Massachusetts

The way Art Charlton figures it, if more people had a craving for ice cream, he might still be in Phoenix, Arizona, struggling to make ends meet.

As it is, he is far from Phoenix and far from struggling. He and his wife, Ollie, live in Westboro, Massachusetts, thirty-five miles west of Boston. They are in their mid-fifties, and enjoy a life-style that fits a couple whose annual income is in six figures. There is the Continental Mark IV in the driveway, and the GMC motor home. There is the condominium at Marco Island, Florida, and the twenty-five-foot cabin cruiser they dock there. There is the 182 Cessna Skylane they own and fly, and the vacations to Hawaii, Acapulco, the Caribbean Islands. There are the expensive hobbies—radio-controlled airplanes and Honda motorbikes.

It wasn't always that way.

Art Charlton—Ollie calls him "Ot" in the broad accent of New Englanders—grew up hard and poor. He fought to survive. He worked hard for twenty years to get ahead, and then the roof caved in. Every nickel of what he has today he earned in the Amway business.

Charlton went to work on a farm at the age of twelve, doing a man's work for a child's wage. His family was dirt poor, and when he tells you they ate squirrel soup you feel somehow that he is telling you the truth. He dropped out of school after the eighth grade to help support his family. Charlton joined the U.S. Marines in 1941, just in time for the war, and spent five years, most of them in the Pacific, fighting the Japanese on islands with strange names like Peleliu. He came home to Ollie, a serious, hardworking war bride, in 1946.

They had something in common—that special something called "grit"—and together they set out to build a life. Using all their savings, they bought an oil-heating business (it consisted of "an old '33 truck and a few customers") and worked around the clock to make it profitable. Four children came during the next few years, but the Charltons worked side by side nevertheless, he making deliveries and servicing furnaces, she keeping the books, and doing the paperwork. And every year for seventeen straight years the business grew. Seventeen years of snow and slush. Seventeen years of calls to repair eccentric furnaces in the dead of the cold Massachusetts nights. Seventeen years of dreaming of warmer weather, of Florida and Arizona and California, of selling the business and moving to a more comfortable climate. The Charltons worked and planned for that time, and after seventeen years it came.

In 1963 they sold their heating-oil business and moved to Phoenix. Their plan was to take the money from their labors and buy a new business that would allow them to relax more, to make a good living without the twelve and fourteen-hour days both had known since their teenage years. Only a few days after their arrival in Phoenix, they found what seemed to be the right opportunity: a soft-ice-cream store was available for sale, and the price was within their reach. They grabbed it. They sank every penny they had saved into the ice-cream shop and bought it, lock, stock, and milk-shake-maker.

What Waterloo was to Napoleon, what the Edsel was to Ford Motor Company, so was that soft ice cream to the Charltons—one monstrous mistake.

By the end of the first day, they feared something was wrong. By the end of the third day, they had that crushing feeling that they had been had. By the end of the fifth day, they were looking for a way out.

It was apparent to the Charltons in that first week of operation that the ice-cream business in general—and that store in particular—had been grossly misrepresented to them. The books of the store had been falsified to show a healthy business, when in fact they had a sick turkey on their hands. There was nothing to do but go to work and try to make it profitable, but it was a hopeless fight all the way. They kept the store open seven days a week, and worked behind the counter themselves to avoid hiring extra help, cutting their overhead to the point that they needed only forty dollars per day in cash-register sales to break even. It did no good. There was never a day when they reached that profit point, and their average daily sales were about fifteen dollars.

So the ice-cream business, rather than providing an

income for the Charltons, lost money every day. They stayed in business ten months before they ran out of money. With funds depleted, savings gone, and not enough business to pay the light bills, there was no choice but to put a lock on the door and call it quits.

During that ten months, Art Charlton had seen the hand-writing on the wall, and had left Ollie behind the ice-cream counter while he tried to make a living other ways. He drove a truck for three months, hauling loads back and forth over the Rocky Mountains during the winter snows. He tried selling real estate. He got a job as a sales clerk in a hi-fi shop, but it went bankrupt soon after he was employed. Nothing worked.

"By the end of that ten months," he remembers, "by the time we finally closed the ice-cream store, we were desperate. We were really grasping at straws. We had that sick, sick feeling that everything was gone. We had blown it! We had worked like slaves for seventeen years to put together our little stake, and now it was gone. Squandered."

So the Charltons reluctantly packed, ready to head back to Massachusetts, where at least they knew a few people, to try to find a job, and make a new start. Get the picture: He was forty years old, no job, only an eighth-grade education, highly unemployable, no savings or investments, with a wife and four children between the ages of six and sixteen.

When people of character have their backs shoved up against the wall, when their survival is threatened, they fight back with whatever they can find. For the Charltons, there wasn't much to fight with, but there was something. In the last week before they left Phoenix, someone had explained the Amway business opportunity to them, and in that bleak, 2,500 mile ride back to Massachusetts, they decided that the Amway business was their best chance to get back on their feet again. It was a long shot, but it was the best shot they had.

They moved into a house in Westboro, and from that day in 1964 to this, have never worked at any job except Amway. They sold an old secondhand Volkswagen to get some money to live on while they started. "We had a feeling that what we were doing was urgent," Art says. "Our survival was at stake. People talk about being committed—well, commitment wasn't just a word to us. We knew we had to make sacrifices. We invested our time, our energy, everything we had." They borrowed a refrigerator to avoid buying one, so they could put money into inventory. Instead of buying beds for the house, they slept on the hardwood floors in sleeping bags. They went to the Amway warehouse—only thirty miles away—every day to keep products flowing steadily to the distributors whom they sponsored.

"We worked at it every day and night. Sometimes we were exhausted—thought we were about to drop—but we kept on, because we really were hungry to get on our feet again. We went when we were sick. We went when there were other things we wanted to do. We knew how it felt to be broke and desperate, and when our Amway business got moving, we didn't let up, not for a moment."

Within six months, their distributorship was providing a decent living for them, and within two years it had become highly profitable. The pressures to survive were off, but the Charltons by now were caught up in the excitement of seeing other distributors, whom they had sponsored and trained, become successful. "We were enjoying what we were doing so much," Ollie declares, "that we had no urge to slow down and play. We loved it. We still love it. We've seen so many people, just like we were, who wanted so badly to succeed and did it by pure determination and hard work. It's the most exciting thing in the world to see those people break through."

Perhaps because they have known such hard times personally, the Charltons have been unusually successful in bringing other people into the business and helping them to "break through."

When they list the profitable Direct Distributors whom they have personally introduced to the business, it includes the list of people like these: a waitress named Freda who borrowed money from her kid's piggybank to get her Amway starter kit. A milkman. A retired government employee. A motorcycle freak with "no wife, no family, and no personality." A machinist. An adding-machine repairman. A retired postman. The list goes on, a virtual roll call of "ordinary people" who proved that the system works for everyone.

The best thing about the business, Ollie Charlton says, is that they have done it all together. "We have always loved being together," she smiles, "ever since we first got married. We enjoy it more now than ever. We spend 99 per cent of our time together; we have everything in common. Sure, there have been some tough times, and we've had some clashes when we were tired and short-tempered, just like any other business partners. But everything we have is a result of what we did together." As she talks, one thinks of the young girl working the night shift during the war, saving for the day when her husband comes home from the marines; of those seventeen years of long, cold nights in the heating-oil business; of that miserable, money-sucking ice-cream story in Arizona; and of the early days in Amway when nobody believed it would work, and, what's more, nobody really cared.

"It's hard for me to describe how I feel about Amway," Art Charlton says in answer to the inevitable question, "but let me try." He reflects for a moment. "I feel," he says, "like I've walked into a great big field of strawberries—juicy and ripe and luscious—just acres of them—and I have a small little basket. There's just so much more than we can take...."

9 Vancouver, British Columbia

Out on the flat, windy plains of western Canada, out where the sky is a high, pale sheet stretched over the Alberta prairie, out there somewhere is a tiny town named Three Hills. Three Hills, Alberta, Canada. And in Three Hills there is an old-fashioned, fundamentalist school which is named, simply and without pretense, the Prairie Bible Institute.

The Prairie Bible Institute is as straightforward and unadorned as its name. There is not much time, or sympathy, for theological hairsplitting at PBI. There is a workmanlike, no-frills approach to the task of training ministers and Christian workers, and in the past forty years the school has sent nearly two thousand Christian missionaries to assignments in foreign lands.

Jim Janz is a thirty-nine-year-old businessman in Vancouver, British Columbia. He is a big man, tall and husky, with blond hair and a ripping, raucous laugh. Janz is an extraordinarily successful Amway distributor, with an organization of distributors that numbers nearly ten thousand. Roughly 90 per cent of his business is done on the Canadian side of the border, and though he is reluctant to talk about the size of his income, he acknowledges that two hundred thousand dollars per year is an estimate that misses on the low side.

Janz grew up in the no-nonsense atmosphere of Three Hills, when his parents taught at Prairie Bible Institute. He remembers attending church "about seventeen times a week" as a child, and accepted the disciplined regimen of the Alberta plains as a matter of course. He married, graduated from college, and settled down in Calgary in 1963 to teach school and give private piano lessons.

Even Alberta schoolteachers must eat periodically, Janz discovered; and on his take-home pay of $218 a month, the menu included beans more often than steak. He and his wife, Sharon, lived in a small basement apartment, drove an old '53 Ford ("it was two-tone: blue and rust"), and dreamed of better days.

Better days came in the form of a visit from an old college buddy named Gordon Ross, who had been best man at the Janz wedding. He was excited about a new business he had begun, said Ross, and wanted to give Janz an opportunity to climb aboard. Janz was unconvinced, but paid the application fee, which was a single dollar at that time, and became an Amway distributor. That was January of 1964. He began badly, and quickly got worse. His sales volume the first month was $49; the next month

70

it soared down to $11; and the third month dropped to zero—which was, at least, an easy number to remember.

But at the end of the third month, Janz decided either to start working at this new business or to quit altogether. His friend and sponsor Ross came by for another visit and, in Janz's words, "... really showed us the dream." Janz took the biggest gamble of his life. He submitted his resignation from his teaching job, took two months' pay he had coming to him, and plunged headlong into the new business. "My ol' stomach began to sag when I realized what I had done," he says, "but I was all the way in now and I was determined to make it work."

Not that he had very much encouragement. He called his bank, the Better Business Bureau, the Consumer Affairs Department—none of them had heard of a company named Amway. He asked for his father's advice and got it: "A totally foolish gamble," the elder Janz declared. His wife warned him that he would have to work as a substitute teacher from now on, just to make ends meet. He tried to find a place called Ada on a map of Michigan and couldn't find it. So finally, afraid maybe the whole thing was a hoax, he placed a person-to-person call to Rich DeVos, and there on the phone heard the first tangible evidence that Amway was real.

But Janz was young and healthy, and headstrong, and he had "seen the dream." He couldn't sleep at night. On the night that he made a full emotional commitment to build an Amway business, he finally stopped tossing and turning between the bed sheets at 3:00 A.M., got up, and thought about whom he would call the next day to begin his search for prospective distributors. He began calling his incredulous—and sleepy—friends at 5:45 A.M., and by the time Sharon awoke had made appointments to talk with sixteen people in the next forty-eight hours.

In those next two days, Jim Janz didn't miss an appointment. His enthusiasm communicated to his friends, people joined him in his business, and his total sales volume was $8,200 that month!

He was off and running. "Nobody has ever really built this business successfully without overcoming some obstacles," Sharon says, "and, believe me, we had our share." The young couple—Jim was twenty-two years old—had to order products from a warehouse in London, Ontario, almost twenty-five hundred miles away, and often waited as much as a month for delivery. The business grew so fast they constantly borrowed money to keep the products flowing smoothly. They operated on blind faith and instinct. There were few training materials available to them in Western Canada at the time, and they had never attended an official Amway sales meeting. "We just threw mud on the wall and hoped some of it would stick!" Janz recalls. "Our business grew because we were selling good products, we were operating in good faith, and we believed totally in what we were doing. We are much more sophisticated now, have a better organized business, but I wonder sometimes if we really are as effective now as we were in those early days when we had all that energy and enthusiasm."

Lest that sound too much like the nostalgic musings of an old veteran, keep in mind that the speaker is in his midthirties, as robust as Paul Bunyan in his prime. He has a charming wife whose smile can warm a winter night, a quarter-million-dollar home in Vancouver with two Cadillacs in the garage, and a resort condominium in

Bellingham, Washington, with a boat and all the other trappings. He has been at the top level (Crown Ambassador) of the Amway achievement ladder since 1979. And he has all the spirit and optimism of a man whose fun has just begun.

Maybe he won't have to do any more substitute teaching after all.

10 Santa Barbara, California

Stuttering is hilarious.

There are lots of funny jokes we tell about stuttering; some of them you probably have heard all your life. Do you remember the one about the stutterer who joined the paratroopers and was still counting "s-s-s-s-s-s-seven" when he hit the ground? Or the one about the two stutterers in a bar who had a knockdown, drag-out fight because each thought the other was making fun of him?

Stuttering is funny, all right.

To everyone but the stutterer. To him, stuttering is no joke; it is a nightmare. To the person who stutters badly, every social situation, every new contact, can be traumatic and embarrassing. He is constantly afraid of new situations, of having to meet new people. There are many jobs he cannot even apply for; many things other people do routinely that become difficult and painful. Something as simple as talking to a long-distance operator on the phone can become a major hassle. Stuttering is no laughing matter to the stutterer. It is a cloud that follows him through life, always hanging just overhead, always threatening to rain on his parade.

And if the individual who stutters badly is bright and ambitious, if he is hungry to get ahead, to do things in life that are creative and exciting, the obstacle is even more frustrating. Such was the case with Dan Williams, who stuttered badly from the age of five. A native of upstate New York, he grew up eager to prove himself, to accomplish things, to have the good life. But constantly, wherever he turned, there was this stuttering problem, always blocking the path, always making things more difficult. When he graduated from high school during World War II, he wanted to be a navy pilot and passed the written exams for the officer-candidate program, but stuttering kept him out. He joined the U.S. Merchant Marines instead, went to Officer Candidate School there, and was commissioned as a third assistant engineer. He sailed for ten years, became a chief engineer with major responsibilities aboard the ships he worked, and traveled all over the world.

With the help of his wife, Bunny, Dan tried throughout these years to lick his stuttering problem. He read everything he could find on the subject. He had himself hypnotized one year on Ellis Island, but that didn't work. He tried psychoanalysis, tried CO_2 inhalation treatment, but still was no better. At the age of twenty-nine, he heard that a new drug called *Serpasil* (which is used to treat high blood pressure) offered an instant cure for his problem. He tried it and it worked, instantly, miraculously, so he took two days of tests at the recruiting offices of the United States Navy, breezed through, and entered the Navy as lieutenant, junior grade, on a destroyer. But, horror of horrors, within a few days the drug began to wear off. Larger doses did no good. Soon he was stuttering as badly as ever. He was terrified! He wondered, "Do I confess to the navy and get out now, or do I try to bluff it through?" He decided to bluff it through.

It worked for a while. He was the engineering officer of the USS *Murray*, and every day was a battle to conceal his stuttering problem. "Every night, as the engineering officer," he recalls today, "I had to go through one line. I had to say 'Engineering department, all present and accounted for, sir!' That sounds simple, but it was almost impossible for me to climb up to the bridge and make that simple report every night at sea. I used to practice that line at home. I repeated it, over and over, all the way to the deck, blurted it out, and went back below, away from people I might have to talk to, as quickly as I could."

Williams obviously could not survive long in the navy under those conditons, and his career was a short one. In 1957 he left the military to take a job with Dow Chemical Company at a plant near Baton Rouge, Louisiana. There his considerable abilities as an engineer could be used to maximum advantage. He supervised the utilities department of one of Dow's divisions and settled down with Bunny and their three children. His stuttering persisted, and he continued to fight it. He tried a speech clinic at Louisiana State University for two semesters, but with no success. He seemed stuck with an incurable problem.

After several years at the plant in Baton Rouge, his speech problem was not the only thing he was stuck with. His job began to seem increasingly a trap rather than a paradise. "We simply weren't making enough money. There was never enough to go around—certainly none left over for savings or vacations. I began to worry about the kids' college education—we had a grand total of $35.60 in the bank. I had always moved up in my jobs before, but I felt blocked from any further promotion at Dow. I thought about selling real estate or insurance to make some extra money, but my stuttering made that totally out of the question. I was completely frustrated, and felt that I was in some sort of trap that there was no escape from."

And so when Dan's brother-in-law called one evening in 1966 and said he was in a part-time business that could bring eight hundred dollars a month, Dan and Bunny were ready to listen. "Just give me a mask and a gun, and I'm with you!" Dan joked. "I'm ready for anything!"

He met the brother-in-law at Brennan's, the famous New Orleans restaurant, and the business opportunity Williams saw was the Amway marketing plan, sketched out on one of Brennan's finest table napkins. He got in immediately, and went home to hold his first two meetings that weekend. Five of their friends joined as distributors and Bunny got three retail customers out of those meetings, and they were rolling. They began to dream about the business at night, think about it in the daytime. They became involved emotionally, got excited about the prospects of what their business could become. Their marketing organization began to grow, and so did their enthusiasm. It was a happy, exhilarating, upward spiral. When he explained the marketing plan to prospective distributors, Dan could hide his stuttering for "about 60 to 90 seconds," and after that, he just buckled up his courage and plowed on through anyway. "If they don't mind hearing me stutter, I don't mind stuttering," he decided, and with that thought he plunged into his speech every night.

The business grew phenomenally almost from the beginning. In their second full month, the Williamses had a profit of $1,300 on a sales volume of $9,700, had become Direct Distributors, and within a year four of their personally sponsored couples had also become Direct. They were awarded a Diamond Direct pin from the company within two years, and were making so much money that Dan could resign from his job at Dow and do the new business full time.

And a funny thing happened.

Dan Williams quit stuttering.

A psychiatrist in Galveston, Texas, many years before—in one of Dan's many efforts to cure his problem—had told him, "When you get your mind off yourself, forget what other people are thinking about you, when you are unselfconscious enough that you could walk down the street in downtown Galveston, wearing a fur coat in July, that's when you'll quit stuttering!" And that is exactly what happened. When he leaped into the Amway business, for the first time in his life he became so absorbed in what he was doing that he forgot about his problem, and it began to go away. "Dan got so excited in this business," Bunny says, "that he just forgot himself. We were totally wrapped up in it. When we brought people into the business, we were bringing them into our lives, and we felt so responsible for them. We loved them and what we were doing, and thought about it and worked at it night and day."

Dan explains it this way: "Before I got involved in Amway, stuttering took up most of my thoughts. That sounds ridiculous, but it's true. It was like having a horrible disease. Every time I opened my mouth I was subject to being humiliated, destroyed. I spent my whole life watching to see how people would react. But I got so deeply involved in this business, and in the lives of the people we sponsored, that it got to where it didn't matter much to me how they reacted, or how I was coming off to them, and before I realized it, I wasn't stuttering anymore."

The Williamses live in Santa Barbara, California, in a fashionable suburb. They drive expensive automobiles, wear stylish clothes, and have rather sophisticated tastes. They have an organization of several thousand distributors, and enjoy a reputation of warmth and personal concern for the people who work with them. Dan is known among Amway people as Mr. Smooth on the platform. To those who have not been told, few would guess that the confident, self-assured man they see, so relaxed and comfortable on stage, so much in control of himself and his audience, a few years ago could hardly say *hello* to a stranger without breaking into a cold sweat.

Amway people talk frequently about the virtues of sharing. It is virtually a part of their creed that "the more one gives, the more one gets in return." In the case of Dan and Bunny Williams, that principle has been doubly true. There are clusters of distributors scattered all across the country with whom the Williamses have shared time and energy and a piece of their lives. In return, they have gained not only a booming Amway business, but a solution to a lifelong problem as well.

The Dan and Bunny Williams story is modern evidence of an ancient truth: Give and it shall be given unto you.

11 Guntersville, Alabama

If you ever happen to be traveling through Guntersville,
Alabama, and develop a sudden toothache, your best bet
is to go by the dental offices of Dr. Tom Payne, 501
Moore Street, and let him take a look inside your mouth.
In Guntersville (which is just outside of Albertville, which
is right down the road from Boaz), many people regard
him to be the best dentist in town.

Tom Payne is everything every mama wants her boy to
grow up to be, and Carolyn is the girl she always prays for
him to marry. He is tall, blond and handsome, a
Vanderbilt graduate, with a prosperous dental practice
and excellent standing in the community. She is a
gracious southern lady with a college degree who just
happens to be uncommonly pretty as well. Together they

have two healthy boys, a gorgeous home on the lake, all of life's little creature comforts—and, well, to be honest, it's difficult to think of very many things one might want that they don't have.

"The good Lord has watched after us all the way through," Tom Payne says, and nobody would disagree with him.

He grew up in Albertville, the only son of a plumber, one of those high-school-hero types: editor of the school paper, student director of the band, excellent grades, and finally Mr. Albertville High School. When he went off to college, it was to the upper-crust Vanderbilt University, where he made it through on a combination of scholarship money and part-time jobs at the fraternity house where he lived. After one year in dental school at the University of Alabama, he married Carolyn, a hometown sweetheart, and she worked toward a degree in elementary education while he was studying dentistry. He finished third in a class of one hundred and twenty dental-school graduates, and immediately accepted a dental internship in the United States Navy.

Their four years in the navy were an eye-opener to the young couple. They spent a year in New York City, then two years in Morocco. They saw parts of the world they had never seen, traveled in Europe and North Africa, shoved their personal horizons far beyond what they had ever been before. "We really grasped—coming from a small southern town—that there was a big world out there," Carolyn says, "and we have never been quite the same since then." When they left the navy in 1970, they returned home to northern Alabama to open a dental practice.

The Paynes made a full commitment to building a strong practice from the beginning. Limiting himself to a personal salary of twelve hundred dollars a month, Tom plowed everything else into office space, new equipment, and the start-up costs of a new practice. He had a full appointment book from Day One, working from daylight to dark to build a solid clientele. He went to the officials of the local Head Start program and volunteered to treat the hundreds of preschool kids—most of them from the poor section of the country. He became active in the Jaycees and then in the Kiwanis Club, quickly made friends among other professionals in the area, and became a deacon in the local Presbyterian church.

The Paynes probably would never have become involved in Amway, if he hadn't been hospitalized for several days in late 1970. He became suddenly ill and was put to bed by his doctor. His room on the second floor of the Guntersville Hospital was so situated that he could look out the window directly to his dental office across the street. As he lay in that hospital bed, frustrated and impatient with being confined, he watched his patients drive up to his office, enter the door, and come out and drive away again, having been told that the good Dr. Payne was sick and would have to see them later. He knew that many of them would simply go to another dentist, and that the enormous overhead of his office operation was continuing, though he was unable to produce the income to pay it.

For a young, idealistic dentist, who had never doubted that the good life would be his, it was graphic, stunning evidence of the vulnerability of his practice, and hence of the large income that supported his life-style. "I realized that there is no way for a dentist to have any real professional security. As long as I am there—and healthy—I can make lots of money; but when I stop pulling teeth, the money stops. That was a sobering thought." When he left that hospital room, Tom Payne began looking for a backup income—a second income that would continue even if something happened to him and his ability to produce personally. He inquired into numerous other businesses, and finally settled on Amway. It was something that required no up-front investment; something he could develop at his own speed; and which seemed to have almost unlimited growth possibilities.

The Paynes became Amway distributors ten years ago, and their Amway involvement now occupies a place of much greater importance than merely providing a backup income. Though Tom has recently sharply limited his time to dentistry, he says that "it simply isn't necessary to make a choice between the two. I'm a better dentist now than I ever was." The difference, he explains, is that he is more relaxed about his practice, not so obsessed with working every moment of every day at the office to pay the light bills and keep the office operation going. "I can practice dentistry the way I want to," he says, "without worrying about making that dollar all the time." He estimates that his income from the Amway business is "at least as large" each year as that from his practice. A look around the Payne home—swimming pool, boat-house, motor home, expensive art objects, Cadillac—indicates that the business they entered to make the future more secure is apparently already making the present more comfortable.

Where does the time come from? "Well, we've made time out of other things," Carolyn explains. "We don't go to as many football games as we did before. We used to be really rabid Alabama football fans—in fact, we missed what would have been our first Amway meeting because it was the day of the Auburn-Alabama game. We still enjoy football, but, I mean, not *every Saturday*. And we have pretty much dropped out of the party circuit around Guntersville. We just aren't interested in that anymore. And I cut back from two bridge clubs to one. Things like that. We still have time for the important things."

Tom and Carolyn Payne are a walking advertisement for old-fashioned southern gentility. They have that warm, soft style that makes you wish they were your next-door neighbors. And when they talk about their Amway business, it is not in the shrill, overheated style of a door-to-door hustler, but with smooth, well-modulated tones that must have reassured hundreds of frightened kids sitting rigidly in that dreaded dentist's chair: "No, just relax, son, this is not going to hurt . . . just relax and open wide . . ." Perhaps it is that style of quiet reassurance that draws people to the Paynes.

In their "product room," the odors of detergent and shampoo and all-purpose cleaners are mingled with the sweet smells of sassafras and magnolia blossoms.

It makes a good combination.

12 Savanna, Illinois

For the Gaffeys—Vince and Alice and Tom and Debbie—Amway is a family affair.

The Gaffey family is a product of the great midwestern farm belt that girdles the American continent. They live in Savanna, Illinois, a small farming town (population, five thousand) that lies on the Iowa border. The qualities of sturdy reliability and quiet strength often used to describe the Midwest fit the Gaffeys perfectly—and so does the traditional American respect for family ties. Vince Gaffey, the father, and Tom Gaffey, his son, are full partners in one of the Midwest's most successful Amway distributorships.

The elder Gaffey couple are Amway "old-timers" whose distributorship goes back to early Nutrilite days.

Vince was born and reared on a farm, and in the depression years of the 1930s shined shoes and delivered papers to help his parents make ends meet. After he married Alice, he went into the grocery business with an older brother-in-law, operating the Red and White Food Store in Savanna. During those years the two couples began eating Nutrilite food supplements, and soon afterward became distributors. That was in the summer of 1950, and Vince still remembers meeting Rich DeVos and Jay Van Andel for the first time: "They were just two young guys, neither of them even married yet, but we could see they were really going places with their business." Within two years the Nutrilite venture was profitable enough that they closed the grocery store and devoted all their time to the distributorship.

In April of 1977, the Gaffeys celebrated their twenty-fifth year as full-time distributors, first with Nutrilite, and then with Amway (since its inception in 1959). "We put a big sign up on that grocery store twenty-five years ago that said GOING OUT OF BUSINESS, and I think my brother-in-law and I were both scared stiff. But our distributorship made good money from the start. In the grocery business, we had long hours, big overhead costs, and our profits were always tied up in the equipment and inventory. So going full time as distributors was a real relief from all that. We were able to work our own hours, work right out of our homes, and our net profits were much higher."

Gaffey's brother-in-law and partner always vowed he would retire at the age of 60, and when that time came in 1969 he did so, selling his half of the business to Gaffey. Enter son Tom, twenty-two years old. "Alice and I had always talked about how great it would be for Tom to be in the business with us," Gaffey recalls, and the timing seemed perfect. The elder Gaffey couple offered their son the brother-in-law's half of the business; he accepted; and the deal was made. Father and son became equal partners in the distributorship in 1969, and by 1973 had built the business together to a solid Double Diamond level. "I grew up in Amway," young Tom Gaffey explains. "I have known nothing but Amway practically all my life, and it's really been thrilling to get to work with my parents as partners in the business this way."

There are many other examples of Amway children becoming distributors in their own right as adults. Frank and Rita DeLisle, Crown Ambassadors from California, built their business with a young family, "in a house where a picnic table was our only furniture, and our seats for meetings were planks spread across two cases of detergent boxes." But despite the early hardships, their four young children, who helped in those days, are all Amway distributors today: Frank Jr. and Dennis are Double Diamonds, and Debbie is a Direct Distributor. The corporation doesn't keep records on that sort of thing, but four separate, successful Amway businesses in one family must be a record of some sort.

In Ohio, Crown Distributors Joe and Helyne Victor sponsored their son Jody into the business, and recently saw him become a Crown Direct distributor on his own. And, in a different type of family relationship, Crown distributor Bernice Hansen teams with son-in-law, Skip Ross, (and wife, Sue) as partners in a single distributorship. There are dozens of other remarkable examples of family members who build distributorships together or separately.

For the Gaffeys, as for most such teams, the results are

favorable. "It's great to work as partners this way," Vince Gaffey says. "When either of us is gone, we know the business is going to be taken care of. We have houses right across the street from each other, and we have it set up so that if something happens to us, Tom and Debbie have the first right to buy our half of the business. You know, Amway has always said that this was a business that can be passed along to your children, and we're one example of just how true that is.

"We love this business, and it's given us lots of things. I remember the first travel seminar to the Bahamas in 1965—how far away that seemed. We didn't even know things like that existed before we got into the business. Since then there's been Hawaii and Aruba and lots of other places. And then when we went Double Diamond they sent the Amway jet to that little airport at Clinton, Iowa, to pick us up and take us to Michigan for Gaffey Day at the plant. We've been on cruises on the yacht six times. You've got to remember all this for a couple from a little farming town like this! But the biggest thrill I've ever had in this business was when Tom and Debbie came into the business, to share it with us. That was just a dream come true."

Gaffey and Gaffey. That's what they call the business now. It reminds one and all that out in Savanna, Illinois, out on the Iowa border where they plow the furrows deep and straight, family ties and free enterprise still prosper side by side.

13 The Sun Never Sets....

Amway may be the most thoroughly American business in America. In conception, in design, in basic economic philosophy, even in its very name itself, Amway is almost uniquely American.

It is one of the curious elements of the Amway story, then, that this thoroughly American business has been so easily exported to other countries. In the past few years Amway has gone international, spreading not only to such Americanized places as Canada and Puerto Rico, but also to distinctly non-American countries as West Germany and Hong Kong. The phrase "Amway of Germany" falls uneasily on the unprepared ear; it seems an utter contradiction in terms. But it is true: The American way is working in a wide variety of places around the world, whether its distributors *Sprechen Sie Deutsch* or *Parlez-vous français*. The way things are going, it may not be long before they translate the sales manual into Swahili!

But first things first.

The obvious starting place is Canada. With Amway businesses thriving in the border areas of upstate New York, Pennsylvania, and Ohio, the spread of the business across the line into Ontario was entirely predictable. It happened almost by osmosis. Before really working toward that end, Amway officials found themselves setting up a Canadian corporation to serve distributors north of the border soon after the small company was launched. There is very little truly foreign about Ontario.

But Quebec—French-speaking Quebec—that is a different matter. Though it has never been technically regarded as an international market, Amway's first real excursion into a foreign area was the development of the business in Quebec.

As is so often the case in the direct-selling business, opening this new area was a game called "Find the Leader." The leader in Quebec turned out to be a handsome young French Canadian named André Blanchard and his wife, Françoise. Blanchard had more ambition than money when he was introduced to Amway: he was working for a wholesale grocer for seventy dollars a week, a seventh-grade dropout who lived in Montreal and spoke almost no English. Françoise came from a somewhat better-heeled home, worked as a legal secretary, and spoke no English whatever. That they were ever sponsored into Amway at all was one of those minor miracles which—like most miracles—involved a strong-willed woman, this one named Monique La Force.

Monique had grown up in Montreal, but had moved to Syracuse, New York, gotten married, and became an Amway distributor. She needed money badly—she had a daughter, born with a hip defect, who needed expensive medical care—and was determined to make her business grow. New Amway distributors usually try to sponsor friends—people they already know—and Monique knew people in Montreal, so she naturally turned in that direction. The problem: Montreal was 280 miles away, and it was midwinter. That made it at least a six-hour drive, one-way. "I was looking for security for my little girl," Monique declares. So she and her sponsor, Ron Schultz, began the long, exhausting trips to Montreal to share the Amway business with whomever they could entice into a living room. Schultz recalls that they made the trip, up and back in the same day, eight times in the first month.

It was to one of those first meetings that André and Françoise Blanchard were invited. He remembers driving up to the house and seeing in the driveway the black Cadillac with New York tags which belonged to Schultz. "Oh, no!" he thought. "This is going to be some fast-talking American with a new scheme to get my money!" Instead he met Monique. He remembers that she struggled with the French language, and made many mistakes, but she communicated excitement through the entire presentation, and by the time André and Françoise left, they were excited too. "I was working at a shoe store on weekends, selling shoes to make a little extra money," André says. "What I saw on that blackboard was a way to make sixty dollars a month to replace that shoe money, so

I could spend weekends at home with my wife. That's all."

The growth of the Blanchard distributor organization was one of the fastest in the history of Amway, and their business is still an important leader in Amway activity in Quebec. The incredible part of the story is that their business was built almost entirely among French-speaking Canadians, and at the time not a scrap of Amway's printed material was available in French. Not the sales material, not the product information, not even the labels on the packaged goods. Nothing. They were trying to build an English-language business among French-speaking people, and the odds against that would have seemed virtually impossible.

"Fortunately," André smiles, "money is bilingual."

The Blanchards went to their first big rally in Syracuse, and understood only about half of what was said. They were learning English rapidly, but not *that* rapidly. "I could understand almost nothing," Françoise remembers, "but I could feel the love of those people. Even though we were from the outside, we could feel the love and acceptance. It was a wonderful experience."

The Blanchards' sales volume grew so rapidly they could hardly keep up. André remembers one day when eleven hundred cases of products were delivered to their home. "We didn't count the hours. We worked until we collapsed. We had so much fun." The Blanchards asked Amway for French-language sales and sponsoring materials, and remember Rich DeVos telling them: "You build the volume here in Quebec high enough, and we'll do it. But first you've got to produce enough volume to make it worthwhile." That sounds rather like the don't-go-into-the-water-until-you-know-how-to-swim advice, but they accepted it; and, when the time came, the corporation made good on its promise. Today all Amway material is published in French, company-sponsored rallies are conducted with simultaneous translation of American speakers, and the corporation employs several French-speaking translators for its work in Quebec.

As the foreign flavor of the French Canadians began to seep into Amway from the north, another quasi-international operation was developing to the south: a Puerto Rican market began to take shape. Puerto Rico is, of course, technically a part of the United States, but its distinctly Caribbean culture, its distance from the mainland (1,000 miles from Miami), and its Spanish language make it a foreign—if not strictly speaking international—part of the world to most Americans.

The first Amway distributors in Puerto Rico were sponsored while living in the United States, then moved back to the island. The population of Puerto Rico is about 2,800,000, and at any given time there are another estimated 1,700,000 Puerto Ricans living on the mainland. Ironically, the first of these distributors to begin large-scale activity on the island had been originally sponsored in New York by Ron Schultz, the same man who had triggered the rapid growth in French-speaking Canada. Schultz spent over four thousand dollars from his own pocket going to San Juan—eight trips in the first year—to fan the sparks of the business there. It has paid off for him handsomely since that first year. There are over three thousand active distributors on the island today, served by a contract warehouse which the corporation stocks by ship, with most basic sales materials available in Spanish.

Among the earliest top distributors on the island were Gerardo and Maresa Herrera, an attractive young couple who have been full-time distributors for several years. He is Panamanian by birth. He had a rocky adolescence in Panama, was caught up as a teenager in the anti-American agitation and demonstrations in that country, and moved to Puerto Rico to try to get his life straightened out. He met and married Maresa, a local girl (His father's last words to him when he left Panama: "Whatever you do, son, don't marry a Puerto Rican!") and began to turn his enormous energy into productive channels.

When he first saw the Amway plan, he was an executive in the insurance business. "I had what I thought I wanted," he says, "a nine-to-five work day, title on the office door, a ninety-two-inch desk, a certain amount of status, one night out with 'the boys' every week. But I really was frustrated and bored with the insurance business. The moment I saw that marketing plan on the blackboard, I knew I was through with insurance."

Maresa—it is a beautiful name the way the Latins say it—approved of the change immediately. "We had very little in common before we got into the business. He would be off talking to people all day, and I would be home with the kids. When he came home, I would be dying to talk, and he would hardly say a word. He was tired of talking! I would have to spoon out a few words. Things are totally different now. We share this thing completely, and it's been great for us." Their conversation is more likely to be in English, too, as Maresa has learned the language rapidly since coming into Amway, and says that many of their distributors have been similarly motivated to learn English to help their new businesses.

Are there major differences in building the business in Puerto Rico? "No, I don't think so," Herrera states. "People are the same everywhere, and this business is built on people. In fact, being confined on a single island is an advantage. Puerto Rico is only 100 miles long and 35 miles wide, but there are almost 3 million people here. We don't waste any time traveling long distances to sponsor people, like some do in the States. Every town on the island is an easy drive from here. Our own business has grown right here in town—all our Direct Distributors are from San Juan. We had to learn that the grass is green right here, and I think overall that has been an advantage to us. Getting our products from the warehouse is sometimes a bother. They do a good job staying supplied, but we are just selling the products faster than they can get them into the warehouse sometimes!"

To the Herreras, that may be "sometimes a bother," but to the corporation it is a sign of a healthy, growing sales volume in Puerto Rico. The business seems firmly entrenched on the island. Besides the Herreras, who have earned Triple Diamond recognition from the company, there are many newer, equally successful distributorships developing, and the growth rate in Puerto Rico has been among the best in the world of Amway for the past few years.

Language and distance. These are tough barriers for a company to cross in developing international business. Though both the Puerto Rican and Canadian Amway operations have an international flavor, they developed in both cases as a natural, unpremeditated outgrowth of the mushrooming American market, and have never been treated by the home office in Ada as a truly international part of the business. The time would inevitably come that an aggressive young company like Amway would choose a target country, one not bordering on the United States, and set out specifically to open it as an Amway market.

The target was Australia, and the year was 1970.

Why Australia? The answer comes from Bill Hemmer, who helped lead the move Down Under for the company, and now is in London, Ontario, in charge of Canadian operations. "There were several advantages in Australia: same language, known to be pro-American, the economy was reasonably good, no import restrictions. The big argument against going there was the distance—ten thousand miles from Ada to Sydney."

Hemmer was twenty-eight years old and working as an area coordinator when DeVos and Van Andel asked him to head up the Australian "experiment." He accepted immediately. "I saw it as a challenge to show my stuff," he admits candidly, "and there was no question about wanting to do it." He and his wife, Kathy, also an Ada employee, spent nine months in preparation, took two exploratory trips to Australia, and made the move in July of 1970. For all their preparation, it was still basically a leap in the dark. Their only contact was a management consultant in Sydney, who turned out to be of little help. They moved at first into a resort cottage in Sydney, the most memorable feature of which was a coin-operated heater. If you wanted to get warm, you put in a twenty-cent coin!

The Hemmers opened a base of operations in a small apartment they rented. The telephone company did not put a phone in for six weeks, and Hemmer conducted his business from a phone booth outside, working with rolls

Amway co-founder Rich DeVos enthusiastically congratulates Elsie Marsh while husband Charlie looks on. The occasion? Charlie and Elsie's qualifying as Amway's first Crown Direct Distributors.

Crown Direct Distributors Frank and Rita Delisle, members of Amway's prestigious Executive Diamond Council, shown participating in a discussion session at the 1976 meeting in the Bahamas.

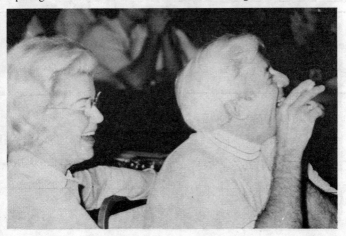

Amway's first convention was held in 1960 at the Pantlind Hotel in Grand Rapids.

The attendance at the 1967 convention (held at the Civic Auditorium in Grand Rapids) was considerably larger than the one held in 1960.

Crown Direct Distributor Bernice Hansen addresses a record convention audience of more than 30,000 who attended two big Amway programs in Washington, D.C.'s huge Capitol Centre Arena in 1975.

Jay and Betty Van Andel talk with distributors at an Amway Convention.

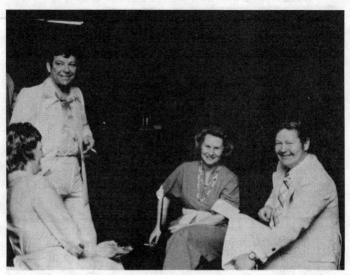

Informal business discussion by members of Amway's exclusive Diamond Club. Left to right: Ruth Evans, Bill Campbell, Jan Campbell, Stan Evans.

More Diamonds in an informal setting. Left to right: Alice and Vince Gaffey, Art and Ollie Charlton.

The Great American Dream Pageant played to standing ovations and critical acclaim before audiences totaling over 170,000 in 23 cities across North America in 1975-76. Pageant performers shown, left to right: Laurie Shreve, Ward Carlson, Dinah Stokes, Paul Wegemenn, LeeRoy Hearn(blocked), Pamela Cooper, Brenda Norris, Dusty Owens, Bob Wollter, Sharon Delisle, Skip Ross, Helen Johnson, Brian Cutler, Ron Stokes.

Jay Van Andel and Rich DeVos present gifts of appreciation to Diamond Direct Distributors Fred and Jan Sanborn after the final performance of the widely acclaimed Great American Dream Pageant.

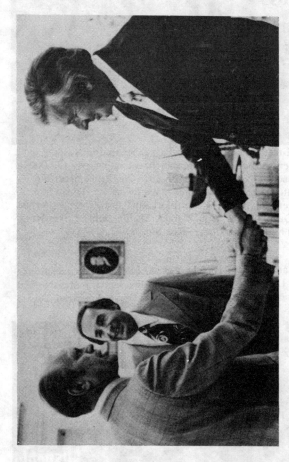

Rich DeVos and Jay Van Andel in the Oval Office with President Gerald R. Ford on the occasion of the re-signing of the Declaration of Independence (April 1975). Re-signing of the Declaration was the Amway Distributors' Bicentennial Year project.

Jay Van Andel and Rich DeVos greet Double Diamond Direct Distributors Heleyne and Joe Victor during the June 1975 Amway International Leadership Convention in Washington, D.C.

Amway's luxurious sea-going conference room, the Motor Yacht *Enterprise*, hosts Diamond Club members at sea the year round.

The co-founders of Amway Corporation are photographed in the board room of the Center of Free Enterprise. For them—and thousands of others in Amway—the possible dream came true.

of dimes bulging in his pockets as he fed the pay phone and made his calls. Hemmer selected a product line of ten or twelve basic products, contracted with manufacturers to have them made in the country, selected a warehouse and office location, hired a general manager (Laurie Mulham, who is now an Amway executive vice-president) and began making contacts with prospects whose names and addresses had been supplied by distributors in the States. Hemmer and Mulham then began a series of meetings around the country to develop interest in the new business. The strategy was to have a long drum-roll before the curtain finally went up. Following up on their lists of prospects, they held meetings in Sydney, Melbourne, Brisbane, and Perth. Interest built. People began calling the Hemmers and coming to their apartment at all hours of the day and night.

When the day came to begin accepting distributor applications, the groundwork had been done. "It was an exciting time," Hemmer says. "One day in Brisbane we had about eighty people sitting down filling out forms all at one time." The business got off to a solid start, and has grown steadily ever since. The arrangement to manufacture products in Australia proved to be a bad one, and all products are now shipped from the home plant in Michigan. The corporation has gradually built its Australian staff to several dozen employees, and the entire operation is now firmly in the black.

The Australian expansion looked somewhat different from the other side of the Pacific. To Bill Hemmer, it was an exciting new venture; for Australian Peter Javelin, it had more the look of another unwelcome Yankee scheme.

101

Javelin is now a Triple Diamond, a leading producer among Australia's twenty thousand distributors. He is forty-five years old, with darting, intense blue eyes, a pencil-thin moustache, and bushy sideburns. His story sounds remarkably like that of scores of his American cousins; take away the clipped Aussie accent, substitute Chicago for Adelaide, and one could hardly tell the difference. He was an eighth-grade dropout who never accepted the "loser" label. He was a jack-of-all-trades; night-club singer, state champion bicyclist, pawnbroker, salesman in a variety of businesses. One year business was bad, and he had to put his home up for sale. The man who bought it was an engineer from Phoenix, Arizona. Helping the new homeowner move his belongings into the house, Javelin found himself carrying a box of laundry detergent. What kind of nut would want to bring a box of household products all the way from Phoenix to Adelaide? he wondered. "Oh, those are Amway products," the engineer told him. "They're the best in the world, and I wouldn't leave home without them!" He never forgot that, and a few years later, when he was invited to an Amway meeting at a downtown hotel, he went, somewhat belligerently to "see what those smart-aleck Yanks are up to."

Along with his wife, Penny, he started building an Amway business that now is one of the largest anywhere in the world of Amway. Ironically, the original promotional work done by the corporation had not included Adelaide, because it was felt there was not enough potential there; and that single city now accounts for 40 per cent of the total Australian volume. "This business is perfect for Australia," the Javelins declare. "People here still have plenty of the pioneer spirit that makes the Amway plan work. Our inflation is terrible. It takes a second income of some sort just to stay even. We get good product flow from the States. The company conducts rallies every six to eight weeks. Why shouldn't it work here at least as well as anywhere else?"

Indeed, why not?

The corporation, encouraged by the Australian experience, turned next to Europe. The first new markets there were two very different places, the United Kingdom and West Germany.

England came first in 1972, and in the beginning proved to be a tough nut to crack in Amway's international expansion. The first few years were difficult ones, with slower growth than in other foreign areas. Amway Corporation frankly acknowledged itself to be off to a slow start in the United Kingdom, but refused to reduce its commitment to that area. "There are encouraging vital signs," one company official insisted. And, sure enough, in the late 1970's the Amway picture turned dramatically brighter, and by 1981 had become one of the company's healthiest international markets. Today business in England is booming. Local leaders have emerged and reached the Diamond level, sponsoring rates have increased sharply, and the distributor force shows the same spirit of enthusiastic optimism so characteristic of their American cousins.

Germany has been a rather different pattern. Amway opened its operations there in 1975, and already its sales volume and distributor force have passed the British figures. Munich serves as Amway headquarters in Germany; all translation and printing of materials is done at Ada and shipped overseas. Two of the company's promotional movies have had German voices dubbed in for use in that country. "Our growth in Germany has considerably exceeded our expectations," Hemmer says, "and I really don't have a pat answer to explain why. Language problems would seem to work against us there, but it hasn't slowed things down. I guess it all comes down to the kind of people who are getting into the business. The Germans really *work* the business. They are persistent, sometimes very methodical, but they have a great appetite for the work that is required to make it. Last year we tried to schedule an incentive meeting, as a reward for Direct Distributors, and they were literally too busy working their businesses to go! We called the thing off. That's the kind of attitude that accounts for our success in Germany."

Peter and Eva Muller-Meerkatz, currently Germany's only Crown Ambassadors, are typical of many entering the business in that country. He was a young graduate student, working toward a Ph.D. in marketing theory, when he was sponsored. They reached the highest-refund level in their first full month, and have added new Director Distributor legs at the rate of almost one per month since they began.

Expansion into Southeast Asia has also occurred rapidly. An office was established in Hong Kong in 1973, capitalizing on British influence in that city and the relative proximity of the Australian arm of the company. Though English is widely spoken in Hong Kong, translation of sales materials into Chinese is done routinely, and the Amway business there is a multilingual one.

One of the individuals most responsible for that spread has been Gary Giam, managing director of an import business in Singapore. His wife, Susan, is a public accountant. The Giams heard about the Amway business plan, and learned that a Hong Kong office had been established. He wrote and called the Hong Kong office to urge an expansion into Malaysia, but his inquiries fell on deaf ears. Several months later, he flew personally the sixteen hundred miles to Hong Kong, at his own expense, to investigate the business further and again urge an expansion into his country. His visit to Hong Kong accidentally coincided with that of Laurie Mulham, Amway's international vice-president, and Giam persuaded him to come to Kuala Lampur to hold a sponsoring meeting for prospects. He did, and that began Amway's expansion into Malaysia and Singapore. The Giams became Pearl Direct Distributors, and leaders of Southeast Asia's largest distributor organization.

In all overseas markets, products are now shipped directly from the Ada manufacturing plant. They are packed into twenty- or forty-foot "sea containers" and go by truck or rail to East and West Coast ports for shipping. Transit time may be as short as four to six weeks to Europe, or as long as two to four months to Australia. Products are off-loaded at the areas where growth has been rapid. Keeping stock on the shelves in foreign warehouses has been a problem—a good problem to have, but a problem nevertheless.

The international marketing effort at Amway is aided by an unusual plan whereby a distributor in one country can sponsor friends in another. They merely write persons in the foreign country, interest them in looking at the

Amway plan, and tell them to call the Amway office in their country. The corporation has a staff in each country which explains the business to prospects, sponsors them on behalf of the "international sponsor" and supervises their activity. When the individual reaches the Direct Distributor level, the bonus on that volume is paid directly to the person overseas who started the ball rolling. It is an ingenious plan, innovative in the direct-selling industry, and is undoubtedly responsible for some part of Amway's success in foreign expansion.

There is nothing new about American companies pushing into overseas markets. It has been happening for two hundred years. There are the well-worn jokes about explorers moving cautiously into jungle areas presumably undiscovered by civilized man, only to find Coca-Cola bottle caps littering the ground in the next clearing! Or cannibals heating up their meals in fifty-five-gallon oil drums with SHELL OIL emblazoned on the side!

But the spread of Amway into foreign markets is impressive because Amway is exporting more than just a line of household products. It is spreading a way of life which emphasizes free enterprise, a point of view, an approach to one's individual condition in life and what he can do about it. The success of Amway in foreign markets is important because it demonstrates that, for all the Americanism that pervades the rhetoric of the company back home, the basic principles of Amway are not so much American as they are common to all men everywhere. Hard work, sacrifice for a later reward, a dollar's worth of product for a dollar's price, personal service to customers—those are not uniquely American principles. They have a broader base than that, and they are the principles that make Amway work.

International expansion, in the words of Hemmer, "is really just beginning." The company has opened operations in France, and Holland, and goes soon to the other countries of the European Common Market. A trilingual SA-8 box (English, German, French) has just been completed for use all over Europe. The explosive growth continues in Malaysia, which was officially opened as an Amway market in early 1979. In a few years it may be truly said that the sun never sets on the world of Amway.

Bill Hemmer grew up in the tiny town of Custer, Michigan, and before his experiences with Amway had never been out of the United States. He was recently in Tahiti in the South Seas, on his way with Rich DeVos to a series of Amway meetings in Asia. The two men stood quietly one evening, watching the sun set over the Pacific. DeVos broke the silence to say what both men were thinking: "It's a long, long way from Custer, Michigan, isn't it, Bill?"

Indeed it is.

14 A Dollop of Caviar

Most direct-selling companies have lived for years with a firmly entrenched blue-collar image. They are regarded by the public as the exclusive domain of the temporarily unemployed, struggling graduate students, or housewives who peddle soap or Bibles or vacuum cleaners to help balance the family budget.

Selling soap on weekends is done by dockworkers, maybe, but by plastic surgeons? No way. It just isn't done. A part-time job is for the wage earner, not the professional man. One may recruit new Amway distributors at the Thursday night bowling league, but certainly not at the country club. The average person—if he thinks about it at all—thinks that selling soap on weekends is done by those who are hustling to pick up a buck or two in the best way they know how.

But in Amway that is changing. In the past few years

there has been a growing trend toward professional people entering the direct-sales market place. They are signing on the dotted line, paying a few dollars for a sales manual and sample kit, and charging out the door to supply their often incredulous friends with soap, cosmetics, and toothpaste. Pipefitters, mail carriers, and diesel mechanics may still represent the majority of Amway distributors, but the company's recruiting records indicate that they are being joined in growing numbers by lawyers, college professors, and airline pilots.

The enticements that draw professional people into Amway are as varied as the occupations they represent. Perhaps chief among them is the desire for a backup income. Occupational security is more easily achieved by a union laborer than by a medical doctor, a dentist, or an architect. There is no such thing as a guaranteed salary for most professionals, and the promise of a steady, ongoing backup income from Amway can be a powerful inducement indeed.

Lew Riggan is an American Airlines pilot based in Dallas, Texas. He is big enough to be a linebacker for the Cowboys. Riggan is one of approximately thirty pilots in the Dallas area who are Amway distributors. His reasons: "I have to pass two physical exams every six months, one by the FAA and one by American Airlines. If my heart sounds funny one time, that's all it takes for them to ground me. It's that simple. I don't want to spend the rest of my life working behind some ticket counter. I got into Amway because it gives me an alternative. If I can't fly one of these days, I have something else to turn to."

There is a group of physicians in Sacramento, California, who moonlight as Amway distributors.

Mounting malpractice insurance premiums threaten eventually to drive them from the medical profession, and the doctors have turned to Amway to meet that prospect. One of them expresses a frustration that is heard from physicians everywhere: He is making more and more money and taking less and less of it home. Malpractice insurance is eating him up, he says. And his answer is to turn to a second job, the direct-selling soap business.

In certain occupations, insecurity for the professional man can take more brutal forms. Bob Bolin was a major-league pitcher who spent nine years with the San Francisco Giants. He was traded to the Boston Red Sox, had the best season of his career, and went to spring training in 1972 in high spirits. One day, without warning, the manager called Bolin into his office and informed him that he was being released. "The team is going with younger players," the manager said, "and you no longer fit our personnel needs." Bolin was stunned. He cleaned out his locker and waited for calls from other teams: They never came. He was abruptly facing unemployment, with no training for another job and a forty-thousand-dollar life-style to support. He turned to Amway because "it was something anybody could do. Even a ball player." He now lives in Oklahoma and in five years has built his distributorship into a booming full-time business.

For some professional people, job insecurity is not a worry. Nobody is more secure than a tenured professor at a state university. He is professionally invulnerable; it is literally against the law for him to lose his job. Doctor Roland Hughes is in that enviable position. He is a tenured professor of education at the University of South Carolina, and is doing such a good job that he recently completed a year's sabbatical awarded by the university. Hughes is an Ivy League blue-chipper, with a doctorate from University of Pennsylvania. He enjoys teaching, but has been able to build a strong Diamond distributorship without interrupting his professional duties. The life of a good college professor is not a particularly strenuous one, Hughes observes, and combines perfectly with the Amway business.

Amway's appeal to some professionals is that it enables them to stay with their jobs, but to do them differently. Doctor Tom Zizic is a perfect example. He is an assistant professor of medicine at Johns Hopkins Hospital in Baltimore. Zizic has always wanted to teach and do research in the treatment of arthritis, but hated to settle for a medical prof's pay when he could make so much more in medical practice. He and his wife, who is a nurse, entered Amway, became successful distributors, and now have the freedom to work in arthritis research and maintain the life-style enjoyed by a practitioner. Doctor Vernon James, a professor of pediatrics at the University of Kentucky Medical School when he entered the business several years ago, came in for the same purpose: to teach medicine, which he preferred, rather than practice it privately.

A surprisingly large number of professionals are frank enough to acknowledge that they simply did not like their jobs, and built the business because they could make more money doing something that gives them greater pleasure. Rick Setzer is one of the most infectiously cheerful people one could ever meet. He taught in a high school where the faculty lounge was "the most negative place on the face of the earth." Long faces and constant complaining do not fit the Setzer style, and it is no wonder that he wanted out. Amway gave it to him. Today he makes an income several times larger than as a schoolteacher, with what he calls "half the hassle and twice the fun!"

Jack Reid was a banker, "one of many vice-presidents" of a large southern holding company. He soon learned that handling other people's money all day didn't make him any wealthier. He saw the bank as a cold, impersonal place with little regard for him as a person, and the glamour of being a banker—even for a poor boy who grew up in a place called Tater Hill—began to wear thin. He became an Amway distributor, part-time at first, and within three years was able to resign his job with an income twice his banker's salary.

Bob Vest's situation was slightly different. It wasn't that he disliked his job—he was a successful Cincinnati engineer—but simply that he saw little chance for substantial advancement beyond the point he had already reached. "Engineers start with good salaries," he says, "but they are easily blocked in. I was making good money, but I was thirty-seven years old, and had gone about as high as I could go where I was." He became a distributor, despite a "real image problem with the soap part of it," and made a firm commitment to the business when he heard an attorney-distributor speak at an Amway rally. Gradually, as he built toward his Double Diamond level, his Amway business replaced engineering altogether as a full-time occupation.

A similar story is told by Robert Andres, who throughout childhood dreamed of being a pilot. He spent seven and one-half years as an air-force fighter pilot (F4's and F101's) before settling in Nashville, Tennessee, as a pilot for American Airlines. After eight years in a commercial cockpit, he began to look around for something else. "It wasn't that I loved flying any less, but I just looked down the road and could see that I wasn't going to be where I wanted to be in five or ten or fifteen years." He got into Amway because it was one of the few extra-income opportunities that he could work around his constantly changing flight schedule. He left American Airlines when he reached the Diamond level as a distributor. Why? "I got to where I didn't need the money so much anyway, and flying seemed to take me away on weekends and holidays, so I figured, 'Who needs it?' I wanted to be home with my wife and kids more, and with the Amway income I was able to do it."

More freedom. The kind of freedom that only comes with more money. That seems to be the attraction for most professionals. Few jobs pay so much that a man can't use more. For Bill Britt, a city manager in North Carolina with two master's degrees and fifteen years in municipal government, it meant freedom from the economic hassles. "I was sick and tired of having a money problem, and I was ready to do something about it," he says. Now an Amway leader with thousands of distributors in his organization, he is still deeply involved in civic and political causes and says his goals have changed "from making one hundred thousand dollars a year to giving that much to good causes every year."

For Tom Trozera, a Ph.D. (metallurgy) in California doing research for the Atomic Energy Commission, it meant freedom "to be able to ski in the middle of the week when I want, to be where I want to be in the middle of the day." For Stuart Menn, a medical doctor who is attached to the Veterans Hospital in San Diego, it meant the freedom to take the job he really wanted to take rather than settling for one which offered more money but less satisfaction.

Ministers are not uncommon in the Amway ranks. One notable example is the Reverend Charles Stanley, pastor of the prestigious First Baptist Church in downtown Atlanta, Georgia. Stanley, who preaches to six thousand members each Sunday, limits his work to Tuesdays, his single day off each week, and declines to approach members of his congregation with the business plan to avoid any possible conflict of interest. Apparently his style is a good one: he is a Direct Distributor in Amway, and his church members recently surprised him with a Pastor Appreciation Day that included a gift of a new Oldsmobile. In another instance, a young missionary named Larry Jordan spent twenty-one months building a distributorship in California, hoping that it would support his mission's activities. After establishing his business, Jordan began his ministry with an Indian tribe 150 miles southeast of Mexico City, and was fully supported by his Amway business for almost ten years, with occasional trips back to the States to keep things going.

Professional people often come into Amway in clusters. Perhaps they are more socially ingrown than their blue-collar counterparts. They seem to come in bunches. Tom Zizic, a physician, has personally sponsored five other physicians who are Direct Distributors, and estimates that there are over one hundred physicians in his total sales organization. The late Tom Hanson, a muscular young Pennsylvania wrestling coach (who once wrestled a gorilla in an exhibition!) had so many athletes in his group that a meeting of his Direct Distributors resembles a convention of coaches. A commercial pilot named Pat Shay triggered a sponsoring boom that resulted in dozens of pilots, particularly in Chicago and Dallas, becoming distributors in the same organization. Alabama dentist Tom Payne has ten other dentists in his group. And in California there is an actor who sponsors an actor who sponsors an actress who sponsors an actor who sponsors an actor who sponsors an actor!

Oh, well, birds of a feather *do* flock together.

There is nothing particularly inspiring in examples such as these, nothing to bring tears to the eyes. It is the up-from-nothing stories, the rags-to-riches stories, that inspire. The tales of the poor boy who makes good, the gutsy little guy who starts from scratch and builds a fortune against great odds—those are the stories we most enjoy; and Amway has plenty of those, too. But Amway preaches that it is Everyman's opportunity, that it is a business so basic and so flexible that anyone can build it—wherever he is on the socioeconomic ladder. And as the influx of upper-middle-income professionals into Amway continues, it will continue to demonstrate that while direct selling can put meat and potatoes on the working man's table, it can also provide for the country-club set a dollop of caviar!

15 No Biz Like Show Biz!

When Florenz Ziegfeld, the American theatrical producer, died in 1932, his last words were duly reported to the press. The famous impresario, who brought to the stage vaudeville's memorable Ziegfeld Follies, shouted in a deathbed delirium: "Curtain! Faster music! Lights! Ready for the last finale! Great! The show looks good. The show looks good!" It is a believable story. Show business gets into the blood, it seems, and once a producer has hoofed and hollered from behind the footlights, he has a difficult time leaving it all behind.

There is a bit of the greasepaint-and-spotlight activity in the world of Amway. A strange place to find the glitter of show business, perhaps in the mundane, workaday world of laundry detergents and household products, but it is there nevertheless. Amway has its "beautiful people," distributors who ply their trade behind movie cameras and microphones. Most of them are in Southern California, predictably, and many are members of an unusual performing group called the Sanborn Singers.

The Sanborn Singers are a group of Direct Distributors—the number floats between twelve and twenty—who perform on-stage throughout the year, dancing and singing at conventions, rallies, and sometimes even churches in Southern California. Most of them are professional entertainers. They are based in the Los Angeles area, and are one of the interesting and unexpected features on the Amway landscape.

The troupe is named for Fred and Jan Sanborn, who conceived and developed it; and they still run the show, he as conductor, she as the group's arranger and pianist. They are Diamonds in the Amway world and their story is much like that of any other successful distributors. It is what developed later—after they were involved in Amway—that makes them unusual.

Both Fred and Jan Sanborn attended Westmont College in California as music majors. They are Baptists who wanted to serve as Christian workers in a youth and music ministry of some sort, and after marriage they found their niche as staff members of Youth for Christ, working for thirteen years in that organization. As they reached mid-thirties, they began to feel that the time had come to move to something else and quite by accident met a fellow named Bob Stonelake who showed Fred the Amway marketing plan. "Stonelake really wasn't interested in me," Fred remembers. "He was showing the business to a friend of mine. I bumped into them, and they invited me to tag along. We went to a hamburger joint in the Edgar Bergen Building in Hollywood, and Stonelake drew out the plan on a paper napkin while I watched. I really didn't understand it, but I was impressed that this guy was a real pro, and I knew I could do what he was talking about." The friend who was Stonelake's original "target" turned down the opportunity, but Sanborn went home, thought it over for two weeks, picked up the phone, called Stonelake's number, and said he wanted to be an Amway distributor.

There was never a luckier accident than that meeting between Bob Stonelake and Fred Sanborn. The young church musician was so confident he was doing the right thing that he resigned his job at Youth for Christ the week he entered the business. His new sponsor called him every morning at 7:00 A.M., and the two men planned what they would do that day. Sanborn spent six nights a week explaining the marketing plan to prospects for the first six weeks, and at the end of his first full month in the business had generated a sales volume of $8,424. His gross profit that first month was "around $1,300," compared to a monthly salary of $420 at the job he had just resigned. It was enough to make a believer of Jan, who up to this time had been unimpressed with the new operation, and the two of them went on from there to build a large, healthy distributorship.

The Sanborns' role in Amway began to change in the summer of 1964. Fred attended the Amway national convention in Grand Rapids, and sat in the front row, square in the middle of the auditorium stage. "I sat there for five or six hours," he recalls, "and heard five or six solid hours of speeches. Nothing but speeches. I was really turned on to Amway, but even I got tired of it. I thought, 'Somebody ought to teach these guys something about showmanship!'" What happened at the end of the show is a tribute to Sanborn's audacity and Rich DeVos's patience. The self-assured young Californian went to DeVos and said, "You guys really need help." And DeVos, rather than hitting him, paused, swallowed hard, and answered, "Will *you* help us?"

And since that time Sanborn has been a kind of musician-without-portfolio and theatrical advisor to the corporation. He put together a group of singers—four professional musicians and four friends—to perform at a sales rally in Pasadena shortly thereafter. (Among the songs they sang was a tune called "Recruit, Train, and Motivate," custom-written for the occasion in a moment of excessive Amway enthusiasm.) DeVos was there and liked what he saw, enough to invite the Sanborns to bring a group to the 1966 Grand Rapids Convention.

That was the birth of the Sanborn Singers. That first year in Grand Rapids the group included five men picked up at the last minute from the local area. They were not Amway distributors, but signed up at rehearsal the night before the convention so the group could be billed as an all-distributor choir. It was the first and last time the group's roster was ever padded with non-Amway imports.

After that first performance in 1966, it was never necessary anyway. Sanborn received a flood of cards, letters, and phone calls when he returned to California. They came from all over the country. Fred and Jan had written the music for that first show, and apparently they touched a responsive chord among the thousands of distributors in the audience. "I wanted to glamorize what I thought was really happening in the field," Fred explains. "I saw all those people out there, just ordinary people you wouldn't notice walking down the street, out there in the homes and living rooms of America doing this really great, significant thing in Amway, and I wanted to put those people in the spotlight musically."

Among the letters the Sanborns received were many from distributors wanting to join the group. The requests became so great that in 1969 the requirement was made that a singer must be a fully qualified Direct Distributor, and that rule still remains today. Gradually the quality of the group's performance improved. They cut their first long-play album in 1969, soon afterwards added costumes, special lighting and sound effects, and finally hired a choreographer to add dancing to the group's stage show.

The Sanborn Singers today are a top-notch performing group. They have evolved from a homegrown, volunteer-chorus style to what one magazine recently called "polish, glamour, and professional sound that would be a credit to any Broadway or TV show." Almost all its members are or have been professional performers, and the corporation pays the bills to fly several of them to Southern California—or wherever the group is working—from their homes in Ohio, Pennsylvania, Florida, and Louisiana. Most members of the group are from Southern California, and many work in the entertainment industry there.

Pam Cooper, soprano, recalls that it was hearing the Sanborn Singers which first convinced her that Amway was not a "low-budget, fly-by-night soap business." She was singing professionally with the Ray Conniff Singers when her husband entered Amway. They were at a rally when the Sanborn Singers were introduced, and got up to leave because "we just didn't want to hear a bunch of soap salesmen struggling with this music, you know?" When the singing started, they stopped in their tracks, halfway up the aisle, and listened. "I've got to be in that group," she declared. That became her personal motivation for building their distributorship, and the next year she was on stage with the Singers.

Ron and Dinah Stokes are a husband-and-wife team who perform with the Singers. He is a professional actor who has twenty-one feature films (*Ice Station Zebra, Airport,* and *The Americanization of Emily*) and almost one hundred television shows (*Police Story, Columbo,* and *Six-Million-Dollar Man*) among his professional credits. She is a thin-faced beauty with seductive eyes who dances and acts in amateur productions around Los Angeles. They met and married while playing the lead roles opposite one another in *Barefoot in the Park* at a Santa Monica theatre in 1970. Like the Coopers, they are deeply involved in Amway and still maintain active careers in entertainment. Both sing and dance in some of the more difficult parts of the Sanborn Singers' stage show. He is easily recognized for his show-stopping tap-dance routine; she is equally as memorable simply by walking on stage. One must see her to understand.

Another husband-wife team is Craig and Laurie Shreve. Both are acting professionals who have busy careers with commercials, local television shows, and industrial films. He was a top-rated TV broadcaster with a Seattle station for ten years before coming to Los

122

Angeles to act full time. Both the Shreves are pretty enough to make a living doing toothpaste commercials, and have those haven't-I-seen-you-somewhere-before faces that one seems to find more often in Southern California than anywhere else in the world.

Brian Cutler, an actor who played the male lead in a recent kiddie TV series called *Shazam and Isis* is also a member of the group. His wife, Nevena, is a casting coordinator for a Hollywood studio, and handles the Sanborn Singers' wardrobe. And there is also Barbara Foster, a dancer whose husband owns a film-production studio in Hollywood.

One member of the group from outside California is Dusty Owens, a multitalented baritone who was a country singer on the Nashville circuit before becoming a full-time Amway distributor. Owens now lives in Tampa, Florida, and in 1976 was the Republican nominee for a seat in the U.S. Congress from that district. He is a soloist with the Singers, and adds a country twang to the Sanborn Sound.

Apart from these members of the Sanborn Singers, many other professionals in the entertainment industry are Amway distributors. Southern California is among the most active areas of the country for the Amway business generally, and it only makes sense that a certain percentage of the distributors in that area would make a living around the bright lights and flashing marquees of Never-Never-Land. One Los Angeles Direct Distributor owns his own production company; another was a unit manager for the *Baretta* series until his death late last year. The stunt man who frequently stands in for Steve McQueen, and who did the stunts for *How the West Was*

Won, is active in the Amway business, as is one of the script supervisors on NBC's *McCloud* series. And the list could go on and on. The names are not household words, not the names of Hollywood's stars—though rumors frequently circulate that this or that celebrity is in Amway—but of ordinary, working professionals—actors, actresses, and technicians who work to bring entertainment into America's homes and theatres.

The appeals and challenges of building a business in direct-selling are essentially no different for actors than for the average couple in Dubuque or Hoboken. Well, perhaps a *little* different. One actor, who frequently worked late at the studio filming episodes of the *Adam-12* and *Mannix* TV shows, enjoyed going directly from work to his sponsoring meetings and demonstrating L.O.C. Cleaning Product by using it to remove his heavy theatrical makeup! The average guy in Dubuque or Hoboken may feel a little silly trying *that!* But with a few exceptions, a working actor is just a pretty ordinary fellow trying to make a living.

With all that high-priced talent in the Sanborn Singers, it was only a matter of time before the corporation tapped the group for something more significant than singing at company conventions.

In 1976, Amway invested almost one million dollars to put the troupe on the road in a full-length Broadway-style musical show. It was a public-relations investment tied to the Bicentennial celebration, and money was poured into the show to project a first-class image for the corporation. A Hollywood writing team was hired to do the script, arranger-director Dave Williamson contracted to arrange and direct the music, and a full-time director and choreographer was employed.

The stage set and costumes (nine changes) were done by professionals from NBC-TV, rear-projected film clips were shot to match parts of the music, and a road-show of fifty-six people was eventually assembled, including five technicians, a fourteen-piece pit orchestra, the Sanborn Singers, and Amway staff members from Ada. The show itself, a patriotic pageant called "The Great American Dream," was a colorful, fast-moving musical look at American history that avoided direct mention of the Amway business itself.

The troupe went on the road in early 1976, playing in twenty major American cities over a six-month period. The production required two forty-foot moving vans to carry stage sets and props from city to city. Performers traveled on Amway's BAC-1-11 jet between shows, and worked one week a month for six months, usually doing four or five consecutive nights onstage in a particular region of the country before flying home. The show was a smash success everywhere it played. Halls scheduled for the pageant always had seating capacity of at least five thousand, and sometimes much more, and in almost every city the seats were filled. In all, nearly 170,000 people paid to see the show around the country, including those who saw it at regular Amway conventions.

For any performer, the best compliment is an encore. The Sanborn Singers were scheduled by the corporation to do a repeat performance of their 1976 tour in 1977 and '78, with a new show called "Faces of Freedom," and the number of stops increased from twenty to forty, including several major Canadian cities. It was an indication, not only of the professional quality of the Sanborn Singers' work, but also of the growing willingness of the company to invest money in getting out the message that Amway is not a "low-budget, fly-by-night soap business."

16 Fort Lauderdale, Florida

To most people, the name New York conjures up visions of the gleaming skyscrapers of Manhattan.

But there is another New York. It is the New York north of the Big Apple, the upstate New York of heavy industrial towns like Rochester, Syracuse, Schenectady, and Buffalo. In those cities, and in a dozen smaller towns like them, there is a hard, mill-town flavor far removed from the gloss and glamour of Manhattan. Life is not always easy in the factory towns of upstate New York, and the hard times of the 1930s and '40s produced a lean, hungry breed of young men. They were men who nourished the American dream—not a superficial, sentimental version, but a quiet, tight-fisted conviction that the system will reward the man who works hard—

that anyone who wants it badly enough can have a better life than his father and his father's father.

Charlie Marsh was one of those hungry young men, a product of the copper-mining town of Rome, in central New York. Nothing about Marsh in his younger days hinted at the success which he would ultimately achieve. He was a mediocre-to-poor student, and dropped out of school after the ninth grade. "If we had voted on it," says one of his boyhood friends, "Charlie Marsh would have been elected least likely to succeed."

That prognosis seemed an accurate one for the next fifteen years of Marsh's life. He married, had children, spent a few years bounding from one job to another, and by the age of thirty had settled down as a policeman in Rome. He was an honest, hardworking cop, popular with his fellow officers, well liked on his beat. To many people, it must have seemed that the life which Charlie Marsh had put together was as good as he could reasonably expect to have.

But not to Charlie. He was dissatisfied. He earned seventy-two dollars a week as a policeman, and it provided little more than the basic needs for his family. "I had a pretty small world," Marsh remembers. "I owned one suit and a few sports shirts and my police shoes. I had a house that was too small, and the cars I drove were always well used. I had been married ten years, and what did I have? Old furniture. An old car. Nothing in the bank. A bowling trophy with the head broken off. That's about it. I wasn't poor; I was just an average guy, working hard to stay even with nothing."

In June of 1964, the Marshes went to another state to visit a brother-in-law, who casually showed Charlie a can of Amway shoe spray. The spray gave Charlie's shoes such a good shine that he left for home that night with three cans of it in his car. He took the spray to the Rome police station, shined all the cops' shoes with it, and several of them asked where they could get cans for themselves. Marsh took their money—two dollars a can, he recalls—and assured them he would get the spray for them. It was several weeks later that Marsh, the money already spent, realized that he must somehow deliver the products he had promised, so he placed a call to Amway headquarters in Ada, Michigan, and asked to buy five cases of shoe spray.

The answer was *no*. "I couldn't believe it!" Marsh remembers. "I never heard of a place that wouldn't sell their stuff to somebody who was ready to buy. But they wouldn't sell it to me. They explained that I would have to get it from an Amway distributor, that they didn't sell directly to retail customers. Instead they sent my name to the nearest distributor, and eventually somebody came to see me and showed me how to get into the business."

The meeting that night at the Marsh home was an inauspicious beginning. "This guy came in, and he was really excited about what he was doing. He was about twenty-four, twenty-five years old. I'll never forget the first words he said. He asked me, 'How would you like to be rich?' Can you imagine that? Nobody ever asked me that before. He told me I could make as much money as I had the initiative for. I told him to show me how, and he drew out the plan right there on the kitchen table."

The Marshes became Amway distributors that night, not in hopes of becoming rich, but "just to get six hundred dollars to pay off Sears and a few things like that." But behind that modest goal lay a vague awareness that perhaps here was the opportunity that could spring the young couple from their economic trap. "I knew that finally I was in something where I was the variable. There were no excuses. I saw pictures of all those people in the *Amagram*, and said, 'There must be something to this thing.' I figured if they could do it, so could I."

But it didn't work out that way at first. Marsh began to invite his friends to his home to see the new business opportunity. The first night, no one came. The second night, no one came. Likewise the third night, and the fourth and fifth. Ditto for the sixth, seventh, and eighth. The ninth night, still nobody, and the tenth and eleventh and on and on and on. For thirty-one days, Marsh asked people to visit his home; and for thirty-one straight nights, not a person darkened the door. "I really went through some soul-searching," Marsh says. "I realized I didn't have a friend who cared enough about me to even hear me out. I tossed on my bed for three nights—couldn't sleep—and thought of all the so-called derelicts who turned out to be somebody. I began to see that my handicap was thinking I was nobody."

On that thirty-first fruitless evening, Marsh made an unusual, moving gesture. That night he took his wife and children for a drive to the local cemetery. "I showed them the graves," he remembers, "and I said, 'We're no better than the people in these graves. Other people are doing something with their lives, and if we don't start doing something with ours, we might as well be dead and buried.' I think they got the point. I really made a commitment that night. The next day, when I went to the police station, I had changed from a fun-loving cop to a

130

disciplined, committed person. My friends could see I meant business; they could see the difference in me. I got their respect, and they started listening to me. After that, we worked at the Amway business all day every day."

Elsie, Charlie's wife, also became emotionally committed to the Amway challenge after that first, dismal month, and threw her energies into the effort. "I was just a little farm girl from the Kentucky hills," she explains. "I was afraid to talk, especially to a roomful of people. But after a month, when I saw what Amway could mean, I got involved, and really enjoyed it. The kids loved it, too. Finally we were off their backs and into something positive."

Within three months the Amway business was growing so rapidly that Marsh resigned from the police force. His friends declared he was crazy, warning him that when the bubble burst, he would be unable to find another job. It was pointed out that his children wouldn't be able to attend the movies free anymore—one of the fringe benefits of being a Rome policeman. But Marsh walked away without a second thought. "I *knew* what I was doing," he says simply.

And so he did. By the end of their first year, the Marshes had generated a total sales volume in excess of one million dollars. Within six years they had become Amway's first Crown Direct Distributors, reaching the top of the company's scale of achievement. Since the 1960s, they have moved south to escape the cold New York winters, and now live year-round in Fort Lauderdale, Florida, in a palatial waterfront home worth almost half a million dollars. Though it has been many years since the Marshes have worked "all day, every day," they still enjoy a large, steady income from the massive organization of distributors which they maintain. How wealthy are they? "Well," Marsh grins, "just say that I can buy just about anything I want."

Charlie Marsh has his slice of the American pie—but not because he was lucky, or because it was handed to him. Amway put a tool in his hand, and he found within himself the energy and spirit to hammer relentlessly at the door of success until it yielded to him. To a person such as Marsh, operating within a system such as Amway, deficiencies of education and social status simply do not matter. Those obstacles wither before the blaze of individual effort and faith.

"I guess my story proves that anybody can do it who wants it badly enough," Marsh says. "If I were a doctor or something, that fact alone would give a thousand excuses to anybody looking for one. But I was a cop, a ninth-grade dropout. People have to look at me and say, 'My gosh, if that guy can do it, just think what *I* could do!'"

17 Chicago, Illinois

Brian and Marg Hays are the cute couple next door.

They're as American as a Kansas wheat field, as wholesome as milk, as familiar-looking as any attractive young couple you've ever seen at the neighborhood PTA meeting. If they've ever had a problem, ever known a worry, it hasn't lined the face or wrinkled the brow or grayed the hair.

Whatever your stereotype of the successful young suburban family, the Hayses probably fit it. They are trim and healthy, well dressed, look younger than they probably are, have three children, are involved in religious and community activities, and always seem to have money left over after the groceries are bought and the bills are paid. They wear constant smiles, and they should. Life has been good to Brian and Marg Hays.

He came to Chicago from his hometown in Ohio as a junior executive with the Motorola Corporation. With a degree in industrial psychology from Baldwin-Wallace College, he was manager of motivation development for Motorola for three years, and he was good at his job. In addition to his daily routine at the company, he wrote several journal articles, spoke frequently at company seminars, and was selected to attend an executive training institute which was to prepare him for bigger and better things. He was a bright young man on the way to the top.

Hays was introduced to Amway by a truck driver whom he met in a Sunday-school class at the Baptist church they attended. Common sense would tell you that a truck driver cannot interest a young corporate executive in a part-time business; but the truck driver invited them to a meeting anyway, and sponsored them as distributors. Why were they interested? "I had always had a secret desire to have a business of my own," Brian explains, "and that attracted me. I also didn't object to the idea of making some extra money. Motorola paid me well—they had increased my salary by 40 per cent over those three years—but we still weren't getting ahead financially the way we wanted to. We thought if we could get into this business and make two hundred dollars a month at it, it would be worth the work."

So the Hayses went to that first meeting at the invitation of a truck driver (with the unlikely name of General Prince), whom they barely knew. Prince seemed pleased—and a little surprised—that they showed up. "Glad you came," he said simply. "I don't know what I'm doing, so this guy is going to explain it to you." And he introduced an airline pilot to present the Amway sales and marketing plan.

Brian and Marg saw the potential in the business, were impressed with the overall quality of the people whom they met that night, and went to work immediately. Their first meeting was a total flop—nobody they invited showed up. They tried it again, and had a little better success. They began to believe it would work, and their business built momentum. Within a year they were making as much money from their "part-time" job as from his regular position. As their group of distributors expanded, the work became fun; and as Brian grew more and more preoccupied with his Amway business, he became less and less emotionally involved with his climb up the corporate ladder at Motorola.

After three years of doing both jobs, something had to give. On the one hand, he hated to leave the security of his position at Motorola. "It had been more than just a job to me," he recalls. "It had been a career, a profession. I was getting lots of strokes there, and I was reluctant to leave." On the other hand, he had come increasingly to value his personal freedom, his time with his family, and Motorola, like any large corporation, wanted his total dedication. "Companies like that want to own you for forty-five years. There really was a sacrifice to make if a man wanted promotions and advancement, and I wasn't sure it was worth the cost in personal freedom." His Amway income had by now well passed that from the corporation, and he felt that its potential was far greater still.

So in early 1972 he made the break. The young couple didn't spend their Motorola paychecks for the last six or eight months to make sure they could live comfortably on

Amway income alone. "We didn't touch those checks, and we hardly even felt the loss. We knew then that we were ready to make a move."

It was a decision that hundreds of successful Amway couples ponder. Some reach the conclusions that the Hayses did; others opt for continued involvement in their full-time professions, with Amway as a secondary income. In either case, there is ample precedent to follow. The choice ultimately is a personal one that hinges on one's own priorities and inclinations.

"That's true," Brian Hays agrees, "but the important thing is that the choice is there. The new business gave us the option—it gave us the opportunity to choose what we wanted to do, and that's the important thing." Has he ever had any regrets, ever wished he had made a different decision? A huge, spontaneous grin answers the question. He smiles so big his eyes almost squeeze shut: "Never for one-hundreth of a second! We have the life-style we've always wanted. We've grown personally. We have more confidence. We think bigger. We have better expectations for our lives than we ever had before. No, man, we've never regretted it—not for one-hundreth of a second!"

18 Charlotte, North Carolina

Every September, the huge Civic Coliseum in Charlotte, North Carolina, overflows with noisy, excited Amway distributors. It is a big arena, once the home court of the Carolina Cougars, pro-basketball team in the old ABA, and there is not an empty seat anywhere on the weekend the Amway folks come to town. On Friday night, Saturday, and Saturday night the hall fills, empties, and fills again with fifteen thousand people for each session.

The annual Charlotte meeting is not sponsored by the corporation itself, but by a single distributor organization, and is one of the largest Amway rallies in the country each year, apart from official events conducted by the company itself. People come from all over the Southeast—and some from other parts of the country—

to sit for hours and hear a parade of speakers talk about free enterprise, America, the Amway business, and a variety of motivational themes. Speakers in recent years have included Ronald Reagan, Pat Boone, Dale Evans Rogers, Jesse Helms (North Carolina's Republican Senator), Rev. Bob Harrington, and a long list of the most popular speakers within Amway. The meeting is always a high-flying super-charged event, and those who attend each year look forward to it with the eagerness of little kids waiting for Christmas.

The moving force behind all this is Dexter Yager, an energetic young distributor from Charlotte who is almost legendary among Amway insiders for his ability to plan and execute such spectacular events as the fall Charlotte meeting.

Yager is often underestimated. At first glance, one sees a short, rather portly man with a dark neatly trimmed beard. His black hair is beginning to get that salt-and-pepper look, though he is barely forty years old. There is nothing in his personal appearance to indicate that he is the kind of leader who can draw fifteen thousand people to an out-of-the-way North Carolina town for a weekend of what he calls "dream building." But it is true. It is always a mistake to underestimate Yager, for he has some special talent for inspiration that has made him an important motivational leader to thousands of distributors inside his own organization and outside it as well.

Yager and his wife, Birdie, have seven children, ages ranging from twelve to twenty-one. They live in a large, colonial-style home in Charlotte (eleven thousand square feet, six fireplaces) and call themselves "adopted

Southerners." "The stork made a bad drop," Yager laughs, referring to his birth in a small town in central New York. They have been distributors since late 1964, and are frank to admit that everything they have comes directly from their Amway business. "I was poor all my life. I always worked hard, had lots of little jobs to try to get ahead, but I wasn't exactly burning it up when I got into this business. I had a determination to make something of myself, and a belief that I would be successful at something, but that was about all I had going for me."

The Yagers had four small children. He was a beer salesman, making ninety-five dollars a week setting up displays in grocery stores for the West End Brewery. They lived in an old row house that faced on an alley, and when they stepped out the front door, they were standing literally on the street. When Dexter and Birdie piled the kids into the car to go somewhere, it was a "ten-year-old rotted-out Ford station wagon" they rode in, and wherever they went had to be free or next-to-free, because just putting groceries on the table was a struggle.

When Dexter saw the Amway business plan the first time, "It made me realize there was nothing wrong with me, that I was okay. I knew here was something I could do as well as anyone. The Amway business came at the right time for me. I wanted to be free. I was sick and tired of being controlled, of being put down all the time. I felt like nobody looked at my abilities, just at my inadequacies. People looked at where I lived and how I appeared to them, at my lack of education, and put a label on me, and I was tired of it. All I wanted was a chance to show what I could do, and I could see that Amway was it.

"My big dream was simple: I wanted to work for myself, and I wanted to make one thousand dollars a month." Saying he reached his goal is like calling *S.S. France* a big coat.

The Yagers are popular speakers at seminars and rallies, and on most weekends are either conducting a meeting or speaking at one, and still work their own business regularly. Though they have acquired many of the trappings of affluence—swimming pool, antique cars, a penchant for expensive jewelry—they still insist the greatest payoff of the business to them has not been financial. "The money comes automatically in this business, if you work at it," Yager says. "But the things we are most grateful for are the personal growth and the freindships that come with it. If money was all there was to it, we would have retired several years ago. To us, the relationships we have developed are way beyond the dollars. The dollars are there, but as you get more of them they seem less important. The biggest rewards are not getting something for yourself, but seeing others get it."

And what has been their greatest thrill, their biggest single pleasure, since they started in Amway? Hasn't it been a financial reward of some sort? "No, it really hasn't. We've received lots of big checks from the corporation, but those haven't been the highest peaks for us. I guess it would be when we got to spend a week on the Amway yacht with Rich and Helen DeVos. That would have to be our greatest experience. Or maybe being elected to the board of directors of the Amway Distributors Association. That was a wonderful honor—to know that a guy who lived on an *alley* could be elected to serve on a board representing half a million distributors.

That's the kind of thing that money can't buy!"

To Dexter and Birdie Yager, that house on the alley, the West End Brewery, the rotted-out Ford, all of that must seem a long, long time ago.

19 Los Angeles, California

Have you ever watched one of those cute kids acting onstage on Broadway, or in a Hollywood movie or television show, and wondered who they are and whatever happens to them when they grow up?

Ask Ben Cooper. He is forty-eight years old, with a smallish, trim body, graying hair, and a constant California tan. He has been a professional actor since the age of nine, when he stumbled into a Broadway role that quite literally set the stage for the rest of his life.

Cooper was living on Long Island, the son of an automotive engineer, and show business was completely unknown to him or his family. A neighborhood friend heard that the producer of a Broadway show was casting for a boy of Cooper's age, and suggested that his mother take him to Manhattan to try for the part. To everyone's surprise, she did just that, and the producer selected Ben and four other boys who were exactly the right size for the part. He handed each of the boys a script with a few lines marked, telling them to come back the next week to read the lines in audition. Ben learned the entire script. When he returned the next week with the whole play memorized, he won the part without a contest.

The play was *Life With Father*, and it ran for over eight years at the old Empire Theatre on Broadway and Fortieth Street. Young Ben Cooper moved in a single leap from the suburban safety of Long Island to the stage of a smash Broadway hit, and the greasepaint and floodlights have been in his blood ever since. Dorothy Gish played the female lead in the play originally, but in the three years he was in the play Cooper had eleven stage mothers and twelve fathers. He kept his hair dyed bright red for the part, and rode the subway from Long Island into mid-Manhattan every afternoon, did the show, and rode back to the suburbs on the last train that night. He made fifty dollars a week—and that in the pre-inflation mid-1940s.

After his Broadway stint, Cooper turned to radio drama and live television. He entered a private high school for entertainers in Manhattan, attending classes only three hours a day to leave time for work. He did over 3,200 radio shows in the next several years, radio shows like *Superman* and *The FBI*, and roles in the live television shows of that day such as *Suspense, Armstrong Circle Theatre,* and *Kraft Theatre.* "I loved show business more than anything," he says today. "Radio and TV were alive and exciting in those days, and I enjoyed working more than playing the games and sports that other kids my age were into." By the early 1950s, Cooper, no longer a child, moved to Hollywood to work in movies. He worked briefly for Warner Brothers, then signed a long-term contract with Republic Studios.

He sits now in the shade of a giant beach umbrella by the pool at a posh Hollywood hotel, talking about those early days. By his side is his wife Pamela, herself an actress and singer, who wears rings on seven of eight fingers, her face flashing in quick, easy smiles as her husband tells about the good ol' days:

"Pamela grew up here in L.A. She went to one of those high schools that specialize in preparing kids for the entertainment industry. She was a singer, had a fantastic soprano voice, and sang professionally with dance orchestras—those were the days of the big-band sound, remember? We met in 1959, when I was doing a *Wagon Train* episode—that was a big TV show then. Well, all I remember is this cute blonde actress on the set wearing a big bonnet, and I wanted to meet her. Ward Bond finally introduced us. We became engaged exactly twenty-seven days later, and were married the next spring."

Both careers flourished. Ben stayed busy with westerns and adventure shows, most of them imminently forgettable, but a few, like *The Rose Tattoo* (with Burt Lancaster) and *Johnny Guitar* (with Joan Crawford and Sterling Hayden) brought some sense of artistic achievement to go along with the paycheck. "I wasn't a star," Cooper reminds his listener. "I was never a star—just a good, working actor." He was also a member of the board of the Screen Actors Guild for seven years. Pamela landed a contract with the Ray Conniff Singers, touring and recording with the group and appearing on his TV special

145

eight consecutive years. Both did commercials for television, and times were good.

Not so good, however, to keep the Coopers from being interested when, in 1970, a friend asked them about making extra money apart from acting. Ben tells it this way: "There was this other actor I played tennis with. We played together for four or five months and he never mentioned that he was in Amway. One day I met him downtown, going in to interview for a commercial, and he grabbed me by the arm and said, 'Ben, I've found the greatest way to make money and it still gives me time to do acting.' That was the most important sentence of my life."

Cooper was in the best year financially of his life. He had seven commercials running in prime-time television in Los Angeles. Pam was doing albums. But they were playing bridge four nights a week, were slightly bored, and always could use the extra money. They went with their friend to an opportunity meeting, saw the plan was honest and workable, and decided to give it a try. They hit it hard immediately. Ben remembers that he held forty-nine living-room meetings in the first one hundred days and put six thousand miles on his car. They built the business into a profitable enterprise that now yields more profit for them than their show-business income.

"We've never been sorry," Pam declares. "We love Amway as much as we do show business. It's opened up a whole new dimension in our lives." Many of the people in the Coopers' organization are from the entertainment industry, and he has opened an office and product area to serve his group of Amway distributors. "Amway has let me grow at my own rate," he says, "so I've been able to stay involved in acting as much or as little as I wish."

A final question—put gingerly to this striking, attractive couple, sitting there by the Hollywood pool under the Hollywood sun, a stone's throw from the glitter of Century City and the famous homes of Beverly Hills: Do they feel that they have taken a step downward, have lowered themselves somehow, to mix into their diet of show biz such a large dose of simple, ordinary soap-selling? Ben Cooper answers without a moment's hesitation. "No," he says. "No, not at all. Because it's so much more than just selling products. I've done that for years, making commercials for just about every kind of thing you can imagine. But Amway is more than that. I know it sounds so corny when you talk about sharing and all that. But it's real. I'm not hustling people who don't want it, but if they want it I'm sharing something really wonderful with them.

"You'll have to try it for yourself sometime."

20 Seattle, Washington

It is not difficult to assemble an eggbeater.

The parts of an eggbeater are large and easy to distinguish from one another. There are only a few of them. A person of normal intelligence—or even less—can learn to assemble a plain metal eggbeater in only a few minutes, and once having learned the job, can go on doing it for hours, for days, for years and hardly even think about what he is doing. It is simple, monotonous work—good work for the retarded or, some would say, even for the blind.

Dick Ossinger is blind. He can tell you all about assembling eggbeaters and flour sifters.

Ossinger was only three years old when his parents were divorced. As a five-year-old he was injured in an accident and lost sight in one eye. A few years later, he was struck in the *other* eye while playing baseball. The blow detached the retina from the rest of the eyeball, leaving him sightless in that eye. It was an incredibly improbable combination of accidents, and left him totally blind.

Ossinger's high-school years were spent at the State School for the Blind in Vancouver, Washington. He worked hard, learned to read Braille, and insisted on taking classes at a nearby public high school, returning after classes to the State School for the Blind. "I knew I was going to have to live in a sighted world," he explains, "and I was determined to learn to get along in it." His greatest fear was that society would isolate him, wall him off, push him into a different, severely limited world because he was blind.

He pushed on after high-school graduation, entering the University of Washington as a communications major. Specializing in radio journalism, he graduated with honors, then spent a fifth year at the university earning a second degree, this one in sociology. And so, armed with his two college degrees and an excellent work record, the obviously bright and ambitious young man set out to begin his career.

Only then did the cold, unbending reality of his situation come home to him: he was blind, and blind people, however highly skilled and capable, are treated as lepers by the average employer. Jobs seem mysteriously to vanish when the blind walk up to the employment window. A 1976 *Newsweek* article described the problem: "In America today there is a minority that is often forced to segregate itself into special schools, if its members are fortunate enough to attend school. These people are denied the use of public transportation and are sometimes made to sit in special areas of restaurants, if they are served at all. The economic opportunities for members of this group are minimal. Who is this forgotten and sometimes invisible minority? The nation's physically handicapped citizens."

When Dick Ossinger was ready to begin a career in the "real world," it was not ready for him. Doors were closed in his face. Prospective employers were helpful and promising—until they learned he was blind. He discovered that few companies are willing to trust positions of responsibility to a handicapped individual.

Bruce Hillam, a young Ph.D. in math who is confined to a wheelchair, expressed the frustration: "After I graduated from high school, I found that society had written me off. My disability labeled me as one of life's losers, and society grudgingly would assume the burden of providing for my existence. To me, a job was the ticket off welfare and to my own self-respect. But society does not expect or require the non-ablebodied to work. In fact, I was lucky when I went for a job interview if the subject of a job and my qualifications for it ever came up. The interviewer was usually more fascinated by my electrically powered wheelchair!"

And so it was for Dick Ossinger. Wearily he made the rounds, answering ads, scheduling interviews, always hearing the word *no* with the incredulous ". . . but you're *blind!*" lying just beneath the surface. And finally he found work assembling eggbeaters and flour sifters—"something a blind man could do."

But Ossinger refused to accept society's labels and limitations. He fought back. He moved up gradually to

151

better jobs and constantly broadened his contacts with sighted individuals. He met Dee, a lovely brunette, at a New Year's Eve party, and courted her persistently for three years. When they married and started a family, Ossinger was ready to take the big gamble and go into business for himself. It was the only way, he felt, for a couple like them to develop any financial security. So they combined all their savings with all the money they could borrow, and bought a small dry-cleaning business in Seattle in 1962.

It was a disaster.

For the next four years, the young couple worked fourteen-hour days, seven-day weeks. Their business was called Economy Cleaners, on 3520 N.E. 85th Street, and from the beginning it was a struggle to make it a profitable venture. They had assumed a thirty-thousand-dollar debt when they bought the business, and that hung heavy over their heads. For the next four years, the monthly family budget (there were two children by now) was simple: house payment, $104; car payment, $50; groceries, $48; gas, $10. That was it. They plowed every penny back into the business, determined to build a base of financial security for the future, but it simply didn't work. The business lost money. They bought a second business, hoping to increase volume for both operations, but that didn't work either, and the downhill slide continued.

An Amway distributor came by Economy Cleaners in October of 1966 selling laundry detergents, and the Ossingers bought a one-hundred-pound box of SA-8. They came to like the product, reordered it on several occasions, and eventually asked their distributor how they could get it wholesale. And so for a two-dollar application fee, they became Amway distributors in 1966, intending only to buy their own detergent at the wholesale price. They began to sell products occasionally to customers they knew from the store, and gradually, almost without intending to do so, they became involved in retail selling of Amway products. An accountant who audited their books remarked offhandedly one day, "Say, you folks are earning more money in this little part-time Amway business than you earn from Economy Cleaners." And the light dawned.

The Ossingers sold their business and plunged into the Amway distributorship full time. They sold large amounts of products personally at the beginning, usually topping two thousand dollars in personal retail sales each month. With that income as a base, they began sponsoring other distributors. In one week, three of their customers called and asked how they could become distributors. They began to build a sales organization, and discovered that here—finally—was a business with no built-in barriers to the blind, no employers or supervisors to put an artificial ceiling on Dick's potential.

Dick Ossinger never refers to himself as "blind." He uses a variety of euphemisms to avoid the word: *unsighted, visually limited,* and the like. He has a disarming way of greeting friends with something like, "Hi, Joan! Gee, it's good to *see* you today!" Strangers frequently talk to him at length without realizing that he is blind. Dee is his eyes, driving their car and doing the other things which his condition absolutely prohibits; but otherwise he is able to do everything required by the growth of an organization of several hundred distributors. Dick conducts rallies for his group with the aplomb of the veteran sales executive that he now is.

The business has brought him a long way from the

eggbeater days. Now, with a steady income that is "in excess of two hundred dollars a day, *after* taxes," the Ossingers live in a comfortable middle-class Seattle suburb, with swimming pool and redwood deck, vacations in Hawaii and the Caribbean, and three healthy, lively children who seem hardly aware that their dad is a person whom most people would label "handicapped."

Dick Ossinger receives letters—sometimes as many as twenty a month—from other sightless individuals, in and out of Amway, who have heard of his success and write for encouragement or advice, or merely to say *hello*. For them all he has the same message: Amway didn't hand him anything on a gilt-edged platter, but it didn't hold him back either; didn't prejudge and penalize him because of his handicap. The company gave him an opportunity, one that was not limited by physical inadequacies, and he took it and made—not just a living—but a life from it.

It was a moving scene, in that packed auditorium in Grand Rapids, Michigan, in July of 1975, when Dick Ossinger stood on stage alone, the beams of powerful spotlights stabbing through the darkness at him. He was speaking to five thousand distributors that day, telling his story. He looked up into the lights pouring over his face, with eyes that cannot see into that huge crowd, and told them "... the thing that has made the difference in my life is that my perception of myself is different from others' perception of me. Some people say I have a handicap. I do not regard that I have a handicap. I will not *accept* that I have a handicap!"

And as the applause rolled over the auditorium, it was an unforgettable, electric moment.

21 The Carrots

The donkey, it is said, walks forward only if he is motivated, and he is motivated by only two things: a stick on his backside or a carrot dangling in front of his face. A donkey will move to avoid the stick, or to nibble the carrot.

Amway has no stick. It has no penalties to impose, no punishment to mete out. No one is in Amway by requirement, and if it becomes an unpleasant experience for him, all he has to do is quit. "In Amway, everybody is a volunteer," Rich DeVos once said, "and if we ever forget that around here, we're in trouble." When there is no stick, there had better be some big, juicy carrots dangling out there.

Amway has some powerful carrots. There are almost

half a million people continuing their Amway distributor-ships each year, and all of them are volunteers. They must be getting something from it. Some of Amway's carrots are held out by the corporation as a part of the system, and others seem to be unplanned, natural by-products.

Money

The primary inducement for most people who come into Amway is a piece of paper measuring 2⅝ by 6⅛ inches with a thickness of .0043 inches. It has a life span of 18 months; it takes 490 of them to weigh a pound, and 233 stack exactly to one inch high. There are over two billion in circulation.

It is called a *dollar bill*. Money. Amway is a business, and the purpose of a business is to make a profit. Carolyn Fletcher says it best. She is a Louisiana housewife, a faintly drawling mother-of-two who with her husband, Kay, has been full time in Amway for several years. "There are *five* reasons people come into Amway," she tells her audience, "and they are the same for people everywhere, no matter how much education they have, what kinds of backgrounds they come from. We all get into this business for the same five reasons... *money* ... *money* ... *money* ... *money* ... *money!*" And the audience laughs, because they know how right she is.

The fuel that makes Amway go is money, and Amway succeeds only because it apparently makes money for a great many people and, for some, a great amount of it. People don't come to Amway to express political beliefs, or to find God, or to become loving, sharing individuals. They come for Carolyn Fletcher's five reasons. In the course of that pursuit, they may become flag wavers, positive thinkers, and any number of other things. But they did not come for that, and not many of them will stay for that alone. Amway works because it helps people make an honest dollar. Take away that carrot, and the whole animal will stop dead in its tracks.

Can an individual make a fortune in Amway? Apparently so. At least that is the answer that emerges from the long list of distributors, representing a variety of backgrounds and prior occupations, whose gross annual income from Amway has reached the six-figure level. The corporation seems reluctant to emphasize the potential for such amounts, and successfully avoids the "something-for-nothing" recruiting pitch. But the money is there to be earned and many people are earning lots of it.

Amway still extends to people that most seductive carrot of all: the promise of making a substantially larger income despite lack of formal education or investment capital. Stan and Ruth Evans were farmers in Nebraska who lived four miles from the nearest neighbor when they got into Amway. Two years after joining Amway, their income was as great for two months as distributors as his farm income for a year, and is "double that good" today. Clare Gunnett was working sixteen to eighteen hours a day in a paper mill when he became an Amway distributor. Today he and his wife Shirley are prosperous Crown Directs, living in western Michigan, with a steady income many times larger than they made in the pre-Amway days—fifteen years ago.

Though there are dozens of rags-to-riches stories in Amway, the real allure of the company is rarely the hope

157

of getting rich, but simply the hope of getting better. A poll conducted a few years ago showed that 50 per cent of the people who come into Amway expect to make no more than two thousand dollars per year the first year. "Most of them have a realistic appraisal of how much hard work this business takes," says an Amway official. And it is true that the money most seek is not the million of their dreams, but the few hundred it will take to make life a little better for them.

Freedom!

Money is freedom. If it buys a new dryer, it is freedom not to hang the clothes on the line. If it buys a riding mower, it is freedom to play an extra nine holes of golf on Saturday. If it buys a plane ticket, it is freedom to travel. Maybe it is only a dollar or two, and then it is only the freedom to eat a steak instead of fried chicken. Money is freedom, and many people who want more money, and come into Amway to get it, are not greedier than the other guy—they simply want a particular freedom badly enough to work for it.

For Chuck and Jean Strehli, Amway money meant the freedom to go to Europe for almost a year, living in the area of Southern Germany around Munich. Strehli, a law school graduate from the University of Texas, has such a solid Amway business he was able to spend that time away from it without a substantial drop in personal income. Likewise for Larry and Jan Culkins, distributors from Kansas City. They spent eight month studying at L'Abri, a Christian retreat in Switzerland, and also report that their earnings stayed up throughout that period.

There are other kinds of freedom that make powerful carrots in the world of Amway. Don Held was one of those middle-level corporate executives who wanted freedom from a job he disliked heartily. The Columbus, Ohio, distributor says that leaving his job to go full time in Amway was "like taking a chain from around my neck," and in his exuberance he threw a "retirement" party for his boss and colleagues at the office.

Recognition

Personal recognition for accomplishment in the business is a major Amway principle. Distributors begin to receive award pins and plaques for recognition at the earliest levels of success in the business, and the process never stops. Every person who reaches the level of Direct Distributor is flown at company expense to the home office in Michigan for a two-day seminar. Pictures of all new Directs are printed in the company magazine each month, and reappear in larger and larger prints as new pin levels are reached.

Every year Amway conducts Travel Seminars to recognize top producers during that year. All expenses are paid for scores of couples to spend a week together in places like Hawaii, Aruba, Jamaica, the Virgin Islands, and Acapulco.

Diamond Directs are recognized by membership in a Diamond Club, which meets each year—all expenses paid—at various resort hotels (examples: Lake Tahoe and Palm Springs). Double Diamonds are recognized by a special day in their honor at Ada Headquarters. A company jet comes to the distributor's hometown to take the entire family to Ada; all the employees wear badges in honor, and a banner proclaims it JOHN SMITH DAY. Double Diamonds also receive membership in the Executive Diamond Council which meets at such places as Monte Carlo and Rio de Janeiro—first class, and the company picks up the tab.

Part of Amway's style of recognition is that couples are full partners when the awards are given out. It is an article of faith with Amway that what God hath joined together let no company put asunder. In all the recognition—the trips, the pins, the pictures in *Amagram,* the walks in the spotlight—both are regarded as equal parts of the distributorship. The joke that a successful Amway distributor consists of "one intelligent, articulate, industrious, hardworking woman and one very happy husband" is not without a touch of truth. In most cases the wife plays at least an equal role in the business, and Amway insists that she receive an equal share of the recognition.

Friendship

In an increasingly impersonal world, people still look for warmth, for friendship and personal ties. You can join almost anything you like these days: Friends of Animals Club, Frisbee Association, National Nothing Foundation, Retired Persons Club, Button Collectors Society, the International Kitefliers' Association, and there is even a national club for owners of Edsel automobiles! People like to join, to meet other people, to belong to something, and almost any excuse will do. Undoubtedly some people are drawn to Amway because it is, in many places, like one big, happy family. People find friends in Amway, and sometimes the warmth and affection Amway people feel for one another can unselfconsciously be called love.

Dick and Bunny Marks are Crown Ambassadors from Minneapolis. She has fought a battle with illness for almost fifteen years. On each of her several times in the hospital, she had been deluged with cards from "all over the world." One time she received forty-three bouquets of flowers in a single stay. She has had people whom she had never met fly in to see her, to pray for her, to wish her well. "It's amazing," she says, "how people in Amway care for you just for who you are. Something about our business brings out the beauty in people."

A pharmacist in New York, explaining why he decided to stay with the business, says, "I really learned about the real Amway when my wife and I got sick at the same time. I had worked hard at the pharmacy for ten years and had given good service and helped a lot of folks. In Amway I was nobody, just getting started. But it was the Amway people who called, who came by to see us, did our grocery shopping, helped us until we got back on our feet again."

Such testimonies are common. A new distributor in Washington, badly burned in an accident, tells how so many Amway friends came by to see him that the hospital told him to ask them to stay away. A young woman in Kentucky, suddenly widowed, tells of a personal note from Rich DeVos, and declares solemnly that "it has been the Amway people, more than anything else, who have helped me get through this thing." A middle-aged engineer loses his job, can't find another for several months. Later, his wife stands by his side and tells their Amway group: "He was a shattered man. When a father of seven is out of work for a long period it's pretty devastating. We have you to thank for pulling us all through it. What does Amway mean to me? It means having my husband back as a man—having his confidence back, his self-respect back. It means friends like you. It means everything good."

The Challenge to Accomplish

The final carrot is an intangible one, but in the end it may draw and hold more people in the Amway business than almost any other. In a day of automation and sterile occupations, many jobs offer no challenge, no chance to excel, to accomplish, to make a mark. A famous line of poetry reads: "Hold fast to dreams for if dreams die,/ Life is a broken-winged bird that cannot fly." For many people, life has become a dreamless, boring routine, and the chance to start from scratch, to build something uniquely and totally theirs, is a powerful inducement indeed.

A thirty-seven-year-old steelworker from Cicero, Illinois, quoted in the book *Working,* describes the impersonal quality of many jobs: "You can't take pride any more. You remember when a guy could point to a house he built, how many logs he stacked. He built it and he was proud of it . . . It's hard to take pride in a bridge you're never gonna cross, in a door you're never gonna open. You're mass-producing things and you never see the end result of it . . . ." That sense of being detached from the result of one's labor is one of the qualities that time and technology have drained from the lives of too many people. Maybe the greatest promise of Amway is the promise of putting the personal fulfillment back again. In every Amway story that is ever told, the starting place is at ground zero. A couple starts out to try to do it, and it is *their* business, with *their* success at stake, *their* dreams to work toward.

Jay Van Andel says Amway's special quality is that it says to an individual, "Okay, work as hard as you want, live where you want to live. The opportunity to move up is here, now you do what you want with it." That is a powerful challenge. For Amway, or any other company, to extend it to a person is to offer him a rare valuable thing.

The dream of Rich DeVos and Jay Van Andel was to build a company that would offer all persons who seek it a chance to change their lives. Their dream was to offer those who would work for it a chance to build their own business, set their own goals, make their own future. That, they said, was the American way. And that is the dream they offer—a possible dream, not a fantasy or a hopeless illusion—but a dream that is anchored in the reality of a solid record of corporate growth.

The Amway business does not claim to offer any person a guaranteed success. It cannot offer an automatic cure-all for every distributor's financial problems. But it at least offers a way for the average person to *try* to make things better. It offers a dream—and not just a dream—but a *possible* dream.

It is no wonder that, for so many Amway people, these well-quoted lines from Theodore Roosevelt are filled with meaning:

It is not the critic who counts; not the man who points out where the strong man stumbled or where the doer of deeds could have done them better. The credit belongs to the man who is actually in the arena, whose face is marred with dust and sweat and blood. . . . At the best, he knows the triumph of high achievement; if he fails, at least he fails while daring greatly, so that his place shall never be with those cold and timid souls who knew neither victory nor defeat.